Content

PREFACE

Community indicators have a documented history that dates back to the beginning of the 20th century when the Russell Sage Foundation provided funding to collect community-level information tracking quality of life conditions in many U.S. communities[1]. Community indicators have exploded as a field since the 1980s to the point where it is unlikely that any U.S. state or Canadian province does not have at least a handful of projects. Indeed, there are over 300 projects (both active and non-active) listed in the Community Indicators Consortium's database of community indicators projects.[2] Over the last century the foci and formats of indicators initiatives have – or should have – changed and evolved based on societal priorities, new science and technology, and the changing role of data in everyday life. Not all projects survive the test of time; some, like the Jacksonville's JCCI, folded after an illustrious 30-year history, while others produced just a single report and vanished, but, overall, the field is vibrant, innovative, and offers a great hope for communities to find common ground as they work to improve the wellbeing of each of their constituents.

The Community Indicators Consortium (CIC)'s mission is to advance and support the development, availability, and effective use of community indicators for making measurable and sustainable improvements in quality of community life. The W.K. Kellogg Foundation's mission is to support children, families, and communities as they strengthen and create conditions that propel vulnerable children to achieve success as individuals and as contributors to the larger community and society. This work is the result of a collaboration between these two organizations, and stems from their overlapping missions. With support from the Foundation, CIC set out to provide a comprehensive resource, based on literature search, interviews, and personal experience, on how to start, implement, and sustain a community indicators project that will help create those favorable conditions for a community, and its families and children, to thrive. CIC's focus throughout this volume is on a meaningful participatory co-creation process that leads to scientifically and logically sound measures that reflect a community's priorities and amplify its voices and therefore can be used to move the needle on community conditions.

This volume goes beyond just talking about data. Data matter, but they are just one element of the comprehensive approach needed if indicators are to be used to improve community conditions. The chapters, which are sometimes referred to as guides because they can be used individually, are divided into two parts: one related to the mechanisms of how to develop good indicators and the other one on supporting good practices that will put indicators in action.

Part I - The process.

This first part offers looks at the nuts and bolts behind the process of developing a community indicators project, starting with definitions and an overview (chapter 1). Next, we take a bird's eye view at the process of developing an indicator project (chapter 2). The following chapters take a deeper dive in some of the elements of that process. We provide an introduction to criteria for indicator selection (chapter 3). We then turn our attention to sourcing, analyzing, and interpreting data (chapter 4, 5 and 6) and including quick guide to data literacy (chapter 6). We then examine the theory and practice behind successful reporting (chapter 7). And finally, we look at the holy grail of community indicators efforts: how to move from data to action (chapter 8).

Part II - The network.

Community indicators project do not operate, nor can they succeed, in a vacuum. This section looks at the importance of building solid network, starting with strong partnerships and on-going collaboration as well as effective leadership (chapter 9). Good communications (chapter 10) are essential to any successful initiative and overlap with the development of purposeful community engagement (chapter 11). Finally, we offer some practical tools for community engagement (chapter 12).

More than ever, in these times of distrust of science and of institutions, we need to convene, unite, and ultimately ignite an interest in knowledge and a desire for change. We need practitioners who understand all the facets of this endeavor and can effectively sustain the effort. We hope that with this volume, more and more communities will equip themselves with information and be empowered to drive change and lead their communities toward a positive future.

PART 1: THE PROCESS

CHAPTER 1:
INTRODUCTION TO COMMUNITY INDICATORS

What are "community indicators?"

In this context, a **community** is a grouping of humans who share a common bond, based on a geographic, demographic, or social criterion, such as a neighborhood, ethnicity, income level, etc. A community is a complex system, itself made up of and part of other systems, each influencing and influenced by the others.

Indicators are representations of trends that place data in context. That context can be geographic, temporal, or goal-based. Geographical context (i.e., a map comparing several neighborhoods) illustrates whether the location is better or worse off than other places. Temporal context (i.e., showing data from each year in the last decade) helps uncover whether things are improving or worsening. Context could be a widely-used national or international standard or a community-chosen target against which the measure is benchmarked. Indicators, as opposed to raw data, aim to be accessible to a wide range of users and should be expressed in the most visually appealing form possible.

Community indicators projects use data in the form of a set of indicators to tell the story of a complex system and serve as a map to guide priority- and agenda-setting for the work of groups involved in improving community-level conditions across the full spectrum of challenges affecting the community. In order to be used to understand, predict, and improve a system, community indicators need to be developed with, and be grounded in, the community they aim to describe. Indicators also need to be logically or scientifically defensible, and therefore subject matter experts should be included in the selection and interpretation process. Finally, because these projects strive to guide and support action, the process of identifying priorities and selecting the correct measures should also involve stakeholders with resources and the will to effect change.

> *We have found that decisions have been made, large programs implemented that have not been held accountable or tracked, so our purpose is to use the data that is part of ACT Rochester to change that.*
>
> *Ann Johnson*
> *ACT Rochester[3]*

Community indicators systems can take many forms. Indicators span a wide range of topics, levels of generality or precision, geographies, and durations. They can apply to the community as a whole or to specific interests and identities. The same project may include objective measures as well as subjective ones. For those community indicator systems that are based on geography, some scale their focus at the block level or postal code level, others at the neighborhood level, others around a geopolitical construct, such as a metropolitan region, and yet others choose eco-regions, such as a watershed.

Community indicators are different from community-level indicators, which are indicators of community conditions regardless of the level of involvement by the community and the intended audience and actors. Community indicators are a product of the community, embracing the idea of "nothing about us without us."

Role of Community Indicators

Community indicators projects can have many roles, but they usually revolve around three main areas: inform the community and decision-makers, engage and connect the different stakeholders within a community, and move the needle on some priority areas.

Indicators can help reveal areas that can be highlighted with pride as well as deficits. Awareness of these realities creates an opportunity for the community to come together to celebrate or address the issue. Measures that track progress help strategize responses through funding or policies. Success is often defined as the ability to improve outcomes, as measured by those very indicators that are expected to spur the improvements.

For example, through their data tracking, the Community Indicators Initiative of Spokane, Washington, noted that their educational indicators were not reflective of where they wanted to be as a community. As a result, educational attainment was named a top priority community issue in 2009. The community mobilized to secure outside funding which was used to support evidence-based best practices in the school system. The initiative corresponded with a significant improvement of on-time graduation rate in Spokane Public Schools from 60.3% to 79.5% and a decline in the dropout rate from 29.3% to 12.4% between 2007 and 2013.[4]

Not all examples correlate as nicely, sometimes because there is a time lag between an initiative and any changes in indicator trends, or because other work happened at the same time, or regional or even national trends are occurring concurrently, masking the gains that happened as a result of the community indicators initiative. Initiatives based on community indicators projects are often multi-headed coalitions dealing with intractable issues, making it difficult to point directly to the measurable impact of a community indicators initiative. As a result, indicators efforts are not always given due credit for their ability to create conditions that ignite, promote, and support positive change.

The goal of the Richmond Regional Indicators Project is to capture economic and social measures that drive action. Community leaders like elected officials, CEOs, and funders use these indicators to make strategic decisions. Funders were really the first to find value in this project, and they have actually started implementing these indicators in their grant process. They say this project is a benefit for them because they want to make sure the programs they're funding are making the biggest possible impact within the community. We're also seeing funders align and use this data collectively to drive larger, shared outcomes.

Jesse Harris
Capital Region Collaborative's
Community Indicators Project[5]

Even when the local impact is indirect and subtle, community indicators projects prove themselves to be worthwhile. Research to identify the impact of Sustainable Seattle, one of the earlier projects to select indicators based on a large-scale public engagement process, concluded that although it inspired policies, its direct impact was limited. However, significant effects happened indirectly through the engagement of the community and the process of developing the indicators. The core group of a few dozen community members who came together to create and produce the indicators, and make sense of what the indicators showed, were profoundly changed by the collaborative learning process[6] and it contributed to turning many of them into movers and shakers in local politics and community issues and as part of the international sustainability movement. For them and the hundreds of participants in forums and committees, the process of debating the design of indicators helped shape how to think about issues and policies. It also created connections and awareness of issues that promoted dispersed action on many different fronts with a lasting effect.

From introducing people to one another to significantly moving the needle on an issue, there are many benefits to a community to having a community indicators project in its midst. For example:

- Community indicators are a mirror to the community. Mirrors allow us to see things that were previously unseen, even though they were right in the middle of our faces. When people, policymakers, and business owners better understand their communities, their attachment and respect deepen.
- Community indicators are a window into complex issues. It is easy and common to look at problems from a familiar lens, be it political, cultural, professional, or social. Communities are complex, interconnected systems. A well-developed community indicators system allows for a multi-disciplinary, multi-layered look at a community through new lenses.

- Community indicators can create a mechanism for accountability. They provide a tool at anyone's disposal to verify claims and understand unintended consequences or additional benefits of actions, programs or policies.
- Community indicators help identify a roadmap for action. By presenting complex information in easy to access format, a community indicators project distils data into a prioritized set of measures that can be used to shape action and policy responses and allocate resources.
- Community indicators help tell a story. Indicators help make a case for desired policy interventions or funding for a cause by allowing people to create a larger, more complex canvas in support of a claim.
- Community indicators establish a common language for action. A strong framework and well-sourced indicators create a familiarity with new concepts and help ensure that everyone within an initiative and beyond uses the same words, with the same meaning behind them, to describe a community's greatest assets or its needs.
- Community indicators can help determine policy change. What gets measured gets managed! Community-level indicators can help identify areas most in need of attention, and determine where policy or programmatic change is needed, and going forward, whether the change has the desired effect.

CHAPTER 2:
COMMUNITY INDICATORS PROJECT DEVELOPMENT

The most successful community indicators projects have several things in common. They build trust and common ground among community members, they are a source of inspiration and knowledge for the community, and they support action and policies to improve wellbeing and sustainability.

A main goal of community indicators projects is to tell a meaningful story that can be the basis for making sustainable improvements in community conditions. This goal requires planning, time, and resources, as well as an understanding of, and commitment toward, community engagement (see Chapter 11). To be effective, an organization must also understand and apply best practices related to leadership, collaboration, and partnership (Chapter 9).

These skills and capacities are then brought together in a process of engagement and action. Different phases of the project need different levels of community engagement. Figure 1 outlines a typical multistage process for an indicators project, with darker colors indicating activities that should have more engagement by the wider community.

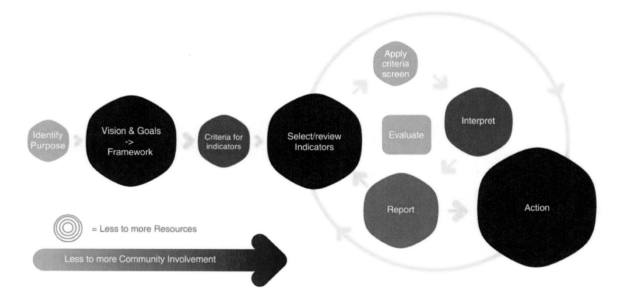

Figure 1: Typical Community Indicators Development Process – The larger the shape the more resources needed; the darker the shape the more community involvement is necessary

Different stages of an indicators project also require differing resources; here, larger shapes require more resources, including time and effort from project participants.

Also evident in Figure 1 is that the initial steps of a project proceed linearly. Conversely, the later activities are more likely to be part of a cycle. The inner circle of selecting/reviewing possible indicators, applying criteria to select a set of final indicators, collecting and interpreting data, and then reporting the data is a cycle that may happen many times in a community. While that cycle repeats, findings from the first round of the process can launch action to affect positive change. From identifying a purpose to selecting indicators to taking action, each stage is described in more detail in the paragraphs below.

Establishing the Project

A community indicators project can develop in many ways and take on one of many organizational structures, leading to different funding prospects. Projects are frequently led by universities, community foundations, non-profit organizations, or local governments – or often a coalition of several of these organizations. Table 1 describes some general pros and cons of projects based in these different settings.

Table 1: Pros and Cons of Community Indicators Project Sponsors

	Pro	Con
Academic institution	Neutral, well-funded, access to research facilities, interns and students	High overhead costs, transient help, not always closely connected with the community
Nonprofit Organization	May be well connected with the community and other community-based organizations, flexible, used to juggling multiple parties	Must work hard for its funding, may carry some baggage based on previous efforts
Community foundation	Neutral, well-funded, well connected to the community, to community-based organizations and to community leadership, can commit to moving to action through grant focus	Internal funders may have other priorities

9

Local government	May be able to allocate funding to project and implement policies related to indicators, various resources for outreach and research	Not viewed as neutral, subject to changing electoral process

Any drawbacks associated with the project's original home can generally be mitigated by building a strong multisectoral coalition. Such a coalition is likely to offer the strongest support both initially and over time.[7]

In addition, when it comes to supporting efforts to improve community conditions, effective leadership, careful planning, meaningful engagement of community members and stakeholders, and good communication will be as important, if not more, as carefully selected indicators. Spending extra time at the onset to plan the effort will help uncover potential challenges and weaknesses before they arise. Once the potential pitfalls are known, a project can build in ways to address them from the start.

Identify the Project's Purpose, Resources, and Role

For a budding indicators project, the first step is an internal meeting within the sponsoring organization to develop a common understanding of expectations, deliverables, resource and time commitment, support within the organization and from the community, and role.

While the decisions at this point are internal, they should include some consultation with the community so that the purpose is aligned with any community expectations. Any of the following purposes (Figure 2) are valid, but projects aiming for either level 4 (providing a community with a tool for action and decision-making) or level 5 (directly involving itself in moving the needle), need to be more focused in their community engagement efforts and their choices of indicators (see Chapter 8: Data to Action).

Although time and resources needed will increase as involvement increases, so do the payoffs.

So, you want to start a community indicators project? Can you answer the following questions?

What are the expectations that this effort is intended to meet?

Is there anyone else in this area already doing similar work?

What is the need for such an effort in the community?

Is my organization totally on board with this idea?

What are the resources my organization can dedicate to this effort and for how long?

What is my organization's relationship with the community and with other community-based organizations?

What role will my organization play in this effort?

Figure 2: A continuum of purposes of community indicators projects

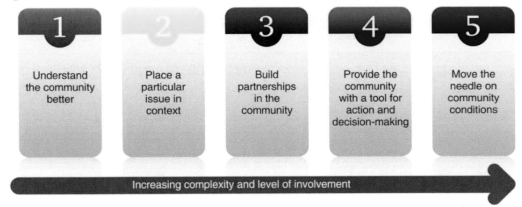

1	2	3	4	5
Understand the community better	Place a particular issue in context	Build partnerships in the community	Provide the community with a tool for action and decision-making	Move the needle on community conditions

Increasing complexity and level of involvement →

At this stage, pitfalls to avoid include:

1) Not having a commitment within the organization for the resources and the long-term involvement that a community indicators project may need if it involves itself in providing actionable intelligence to the community;

2) Not having the standing in, and connections to, the community and other organizations within the community to build the movement necessary to identify, and move the needle on, issues that matter;

3) Not understanding that data, in and by itself, does not move mountains; it takes meaningful data, great communication skills, leadership, collaboration, and partnerships for data to become actionable.

Oversight and Engagement

Thinking of who will be engaged when and in what role is part of the initial planning process. Critical to the success of an indicator project is the ability to engage the community and stakeholders and assemble and keep together groups with specific roles and associations. This will define and support the community engagement process, the strength of partnerships and collaboration, and the leadership role of the initiating organization. Engagement can happen in ad-hoc, one-time events or long-term, recurring service to the project; here we describe key components of both approaches.

11

ROLES FOR COMMUNITY ENGAGEMENT

Community participation is a core element of a community indicators project, but different contributions can be expected from different types of people. In planning a project, consideration should be given to the following four types of participants and how they will be identified and engaged.

Community Members: Community members live, work, or play in the community and have a vested interest in its welfare. They contribute to its asset base and are affected by its issues. Community members help shape the project.

Among community members, there is usually a small group of people who are used to participating in public forums and to contributing ideas and feedback. While the contributions of these "frequent fliers" should be welcomed, measures must be taken to reach out to those who are usually not heard.

ESTABLISH A TEAM TO SPEARHEAD THE COMMUNITY ENGAGEMENT PROCESS.

Responsibilities could include:

- Selecting tools for gathering community views (e.g., surveys, evening meetings, focus groups)
- Identifying tools and places to advertise the effort
- Developing background information to present to the community
- Designing criteria for evaluation of the engagement process
- Reviewing progress and making recommendations

Regular engagement and reporting updates and findings are necessary to keep the community feeling connected and involved in shaping its own future.

Stakeholders: While it can be argued that all community members hold a stake in the future of their community, we use stakeholder here to distinguish those with a specific direct or indirect interest or concern about something in the community. As such, they also include people who may not be community residents, but who have jurisdiction, investments, or other interests in the community, such as funders, local non-profits, or government officials.

Because of the stake they hold in the community, they bring a wealth of knowledge and some solutions to the process. They also have strong opinions and may know the system better than other community members. As a result, they can drown out the voices from community members if measures are not taken to amplify quieter voices.

We think it's absolutely critical to engage the public. It's very time-consuming – and it really makes those projects more of a craft than an automated process – but it is well worth it.

Patrick Jones
Community Indicators
Initiative of Spokane[8]

12

Identifying and involving stakeholders from the get-go is key to the success of an initiative and they belong in the visioning process, on steering committees, as subject matter experts, and in indicator groups.

Subject Matter Experts: A subject-matter expert (SME), usually associated with government, industry, research, or the nonprofit sector, is an authority in a particular area, domain or topic, rather than on the community (e.g., an ecologist or a mental health specialist).

SMEs are particularly important during the indicator selection process where they can contribute scientific or technical background to ensure that the indicator is logically connected to the goal or priority and that it is scientifically and technically sound. Their scientifically- or technically-informed views balance the practical, on-the-ground life experiences of community members and the advocacy tendencies of stakeholders.

Staff: Staff (and board members) from the initiating organization are key to the organization and implementation of the project and should be involved in all stages of development. However, they need to involve themselves thoughtfully, as supporters, organizers, promoters, and enablers, helping the process along, while applying good principles of leadership and collaboration.

FORMALIZED ENGAGEMENT

Throughout the life of the project, the people identified above should be assembled into a few core groups based on their general knowledge and their willingness to invest time to drive the process forward. Thus, a first step should be to identify the groups that will be needed and clarify the committees' responsibilities. Three common groups are described below. Even when working with these curated groups, it will be important to continue to draw on other collaborations and a broad community base.

Steering (or Advisory) Committee: A steering committee has more decision-making authority than an advisory group (corresponding to "collaborate" vs. "consult" on the IAP2 chart of public participation[9] - see Chapter 11: Community Engagement) and is therefore recommended. Steering Committees do not manage (i.e., implement the work); they provide direction. The biggest challenge in assembling the committee is in ensuring that this committee of about 8-15 people still represents the demographic makeup of the community while including certain key players. Depending on the focus of the indicator project, these may include: officials from local agencies and elected officials, education, healthcare and social service providers, community organizations, businesses, faith communities, and community members at-large. Once this committee is established, the members should create a workplan (or charter) that outlines (a) the scope of the work to be done by the committee, (b) its authority, and (c) its decision-making process. The Steering Committee can propose subcommittees to take on particular areas, such as funding, or communications. As illustrated in Figure 3, the Steering Committee should exist for the duration of the project.

Technical Committee: Indicators projects rely on acquiring and analyzing data. Given that not all staff or community members have such skills, a separate research or technical committee made up of a handful of community members with technical expertise and technical SMEs is useful. These technical committee members can provide ideas and oversight of the technical process (e.g., identifying technology and data sources). Technical committee members could include statisticians, academics, consultants, evaluators, government experts, and researchers.[10]

Indicator Workshops/Indicator Groups: When the time comes to select indicators, groups made up of community members, stakeholders, and SMEs can be formed around each domain or priority area to identify possible measures. Each of those groups should include a cross-section of community members, some key stakeholders and subject matter experts (SMEs) whose expertise include the domain. In addition, the group should include SMEs with general knowledge who can help understand the systemic nature of the community. The same indicator groups could then be invited in the next stage to initiate, support, and/or oversee the process of moving from data to action.

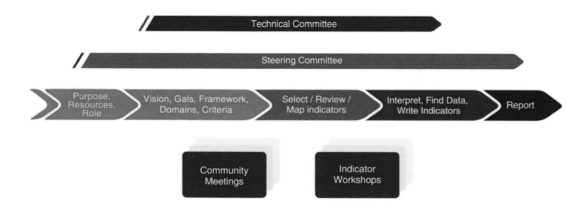

Figure 3: Formalized Engagement timeline – Steering and Technical Committees are established groups that will meet for all or most stages of the indicator development process while multiple Community Meetings and Indicator Workshops can happen around the same short period of time, involving different people.

Careful planning of meetings in regard to their frequency, content, duration, and outcome will keep volunteers (e.g., members of the steering committee, technical advisory groups or indicator teams) involved longer and more meaningfully. Most importantly, people will stay engaged if they feel truly heard and respected.

Vision & Goal

It is neither advisable, nor even feasible, for a community indicators projects to track everything that can be measured. The goal is to develop indicators that can be used for and by the community to map a course of action or to support decision-making. A good first step in the process of developing a community indicators project is gathering the community, or at least the main project stakeholders, for a process of "visioning."[11] The visioning process engages the community in answering the question "where do we want to be?"[12] Once a community develops a shared vision, the indicators project can proceed with that vision as a guiding light. Having a

common vision sets the stage for the development of an indicators project that meets the needs of the community and will be used to inform future decisions.

Any discussion of a vision is likely to include an assessment of a community's current state – both its needs and its strengths. Focusing on community assets will shift the focus from known problems to untapped resources and potential. Community goals and/or priority areas should also emerge from this process and should be the foundation for the selection of indicators. Whatever the process and the format, the product should answer the question: *what matters to this community*?

Data that already exist and may point to some characteristics of the community should be shared with the group to inform deliberation. An assessment of "forces of change" (i.e., factors that currently or potentially transform the community, such as demographic, economic, or policy changes) will also help understand how the shape of the future in the community[13]. Also, note that different groups in the community may already have articulated their own visions or goals and that these diverse visions should be aggregated into a powerful vision statement or a series of goals or priorities for the future of the community.

Indicator Planning and Selection

FRAMEWORK

A **framework** is a system for organizing the indicators under a set of domains. Domains are broad areas that will serve as the support structure on which indicators will be hung. The domains relate directly to the themes put forth in the vision and goals. An existing framework can be used as a starting point for a community discussion or as a way to check for gaps in the community vision.

Multiple frameworks exist in the area of sustainability, which focuses on meeting the needs of the present without compromising the ability of future generations to meet their needs. Some of these frameworks are variations on the "triple bottom line" concept, grouping indicators into categories such as *environment, economy,* and *equity,* or *people, planet, profit.* Also associated with sustainability are variations on the four basic types of capital – human, social, built, and natural – in a framework that is useful to tracking well-being at the community level. This framework attempts to give value to areas not usually monetized. Cultural, political, and financial capitals were later added[14] to constitute a complete community capitals framework.

More recently, wellbeing frameworks that center on the individual and emphasize physical and mental health, including happiness, are being developed in many countries. The Australian National Development Index, organized around 12 domains ranging from *community and regional life* to *subjective wellbeing and life satisfaction,* is the view of over half a million Australians on what matters and a holistic, integrated approach to measuring wellbeing.

Similarly, the development of eight domains for the Canadian Index of Wellbeing started with listening to Canadians talk about what is important to the quality of their lives.[15] The United Nation's Sustainable Development Goals[16] offer a broad range of social development issues, such as poverty, hunger, health, education, climate change, gender equality, water, sanitation, energy, environment, and social justice. Healthy People 2020[17] proposes a "place-based" organizing framework, reflecting five key areas of social determinants of health (SDOH), including: economic stability, education, social and community context, health and health care, neighborhood and built environment.

Selection of a particular framework, whether based on an existing framework or on a set of goals, should be done thoughtfully and methodically because it sets the stage for the selection of indicators. While domains such as Education, Health, Safety, or Mobility are common among

indicators projects and are basic elements of life in a community, others, such Arts & Culture, Equity and Social Justice, Innovation, Technology, or Ecology may be more important to some communities than others. Using goals as domains, (e.g., Clean and Sufficient Water for All, Healthy Children, Affordable Quality Housing) demonstrates a commitment to realizing those aspirations.

CRITERIA FOR INDICATOR SELECTION

In preparing to select indicators, it is useful to consider factors such as relevance, strength, and availability of data and a suite of other criteria that are either necessary or desirable (see Chapter 3 for more details). These selection criteria are like a strainer; those indicators that are appropriate candidates for the project will be kept, while other indicators that are not a good fit will be eliminated.

At this time, it is helpful to engage the Steering Committee in discussions around the scientific and logical requirements as well as the technological implications and the resource needs that specific criteria will impose on the indicator selection process. Beyond those criteria that are essential to any project (e.g., reliable), the Steering Committee is often responsible for deciding which criteria to choose for a particular indicators project.

INDICATOR SELECTION AND MAPPING

Once the goals of the community have been articulated into a framework, the next stage is to figure out how to track those goals (or domains). Different approaches can be used to select the indicators, but all of them should involve a mix of community members, steering committee members, subject matter experts, and stakeholders organized in groups broken out by domain.

For example, an indicator group convened to select indicators under the domain Education could include community members who are parents, youths, stakeholders such as foundations with a focus on education or children, daycare, school district and higher education administrators, local officials, teachers, career specialists and SMEs such as educational researchers, urban planners, economists, and policy analysts.

Domain/Dimension/Indicator

In one approach, workshop participants may be first asked to identify dimensions within the domain. **Dimensions**, also called areas of interest, are like sub-categories. For example, air quality, land use, and water quality might be dimensions within a domain called Environmental Quality. Next, the group can discuss the various facets of each dimension (e.g., water quality may be about streams, or oceans, and from the perspective of aquatic life or concerns about human health, with each of those areas requiring different indicators). These topical groups work to understand the causal relationship between individual measures and goals. Best available science or practices should be used to link measures to goals or priorities.

 We present a menu of indicators that we know exist, that are well sourced, that are viable and reputable, and then have a conversation with the [assembly] participants to augment or amend the list. Then, because we usually don't have enough time for a vote, but we strongly believe that it's needed to be voted on, we follow up with an online voting mechanism. We scrupulously respect the vote of those folks who have come to the meeting and said: "that is how we would like to measure our community."

*Patrick Jones
Community Indicators Initiative
of Spokane[18]*

17

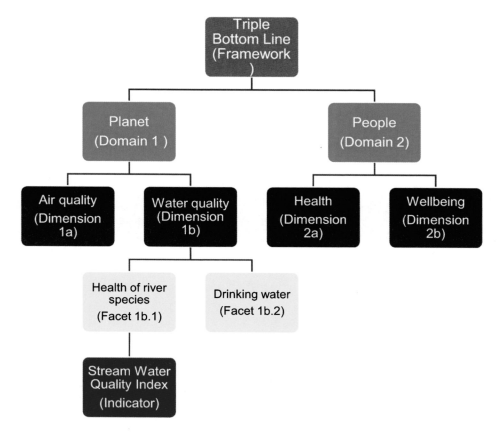

Figure 4 Example of the hierarchy between frameworks, domains, and dimensions. The full model would have other domains, dimensions, and facets.

For each proposed indicator, these questions should be answered to the best of the knowledge of the participants:

- How does this indicator relate to the domain or goal?
- What is the strength of the research associating the indicator with the domain or goal?
- Does this indicator measure an input, output, or outcome?
- Are data available for this indicator?
- How often could this indicator be updated?
- Can anything be done to move the needle on this indicator?

The final list could include 4-10 indicators per domain and emphasize leading (actionable) indicators that show why action matters.

Status/Cause/Effect Indicators

Another approach is to identify indicators that reflect the flow between status (what is happening), cause (why is it happening) and effect (why it matters) (Figure 5). This less traditional approach will result in a fluid dashboard with a higher number of indicators. Organizing these indicators as a network can powerfully demonstrate cause and effect and show linkages between seemingly unconnected areas (e.g., educational attainment influencing both health and the economy).

Figure 5. Connection between cause, status, and effect indicators.

This network is also useful in showing how some activities or policies can be both cause and effect and in demonstrating how intertwined issues can be. It could be argued, for example, that air quality (an indicator in the Environment domain) is an effect of transportation choices (in the Mobility domain), itself and effect of housing affordability (in Housing) and that housing affordability depends on land availability (Environment), the strength of the economy (Economy), the job market (Employment). It can also be argued that housing affordability effects the job market.

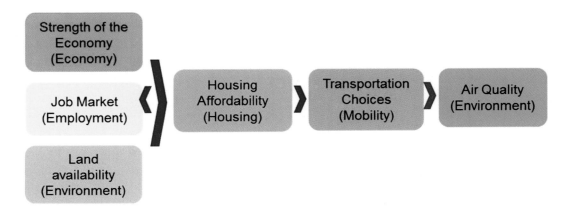

Figure 6. Example of a portion of an interconnected network of status/cause/effect indicators.

In this process, each group is presented with an extensive list of what could be measured under the goal or domain. Then, the groups engage in a discussion of how measures logically relate to one another to infer causal relationships. Indicators that don't fit in to the network that the group establishes should not be included.

Interpreting Indicators

The work of developing individual indicators involves researching the scientific strength of the indicator, sourcing the data, developing the background information (metadata), and deciding how to present it. We refer to this collection of activities as interpreting indicators (Figure 1 at the beginning of the chapter).

Understanding what needs to be measured and knowing how to measure it requires a combination of skills in data analysis and communications tools. A technical group or committee can provide a useful perspective and can help make some of the general decisions, such as the type of presentation that makes the data accessible to its audience (e.g., bar graph, pie chart, map, video, infographic). There should be some consistency on how to the data is presented across all indicators. Some of the initial review may have happened during the indicator selection process, and some questions (i.e., scale, format) may be settled by the choice of criteria. However, for questions left unanswered in those parts of the process, a technical committee's input and guidance is valuable.

A technical committee may also provide support in sourcing or even analyzing data. Other approaches for increasing data analytic capacity in team that is small or not data-savvy include adding someone with these skills to the project, outsourcing the analysis to a consultant or academic partner, or partnering with another agency who does have staff with this technical capacity. In Chapter 5 and 6, we cover the basics of data analysis and common sources of indicator data.

In addition to the raw data, each indicator needs background information (metadata) in the form of a few paragraphs that explains why it matters and how it relates to the vision or the goal/domain. The metadata should also include details about the source and timing of the data and any information related to its strengths or limitations. Being clear about that this information is necessary for transparency, use, and building an organizational memory of decisions and knowledge that can outlast any particular person in the event of changes in personnel.

Some indicators may not survive this stage, particularly if strict criteria exist about the source of the data or the resources involved in obtaining it. It may be necessary to go back to the work of the Indicator Selection process to better understand the intentions behind the selection and propose other measures that could meet the same intention.

Post Indicator Work

REPORTING

The medium used to report the indicators depends on the intended audience and should be chosen carefully after consultations with the community. Even perfectly selected indicators presented in a detailed format will be a waste unless that product can attract and engage audience members. A beautiful report is useless without interested readers.

The same set of indicators can – and often should – be reported in multiple different formats (e.g., online for researchers, through a newspaper insert for the community, and as one-page scorecard for elected officials). For a more in-depth discussion of such approaches, please refer to Chapter 7.

Our indicator project has gone through a lot of transitions in responses to changes both locally and globally over the last 30 years, not the least of which has been the internet. The report used to be published as a large document, very detailed; now we publish a simple trifold document, like an executive summary, and we publish our indicators on a web-based, interactive platform.

Susan Cohn
JCCI Quality of Life Report[19]

When we aligned our report with [community priorities], it became clear that we needed to provide a way for residents to become more instrumental in community change and we needed to frame our message more directly through the lens of action. So, we restructured our message to the community as a call to action

Susan Cohn
JCCI[20]

Additionally, there is a face-to-face component to reporting that should not be underestimated. Presenting the report, or dashboard, to the community, local officials, and community-based organizations, to name just a few, will ensure dissemination of the information and a strengthening of relationships that will lead to more intensive use of the data. Such interactive events allow for a back-and-forth dialog about the indicators that benefits both the producers and audience of the report or dashboard.

EVALUATION

Periodic evaluation of an indicators project is key to its sustainability, longevity, and, most importantly, its relevance. **Evaluation** is the process of collecting and summarizing evidence that leads to conclusions about the value, merit, significance or quality of an effort.[20]

Process evaluations are just that – an evaluation of the project's processes. They may look at things like the number of community events held, the number of subject matter experts engaged, the number of data partnerships formed – things that can suggest if a project is on a good trajectory, even if it is too soon to expect the needle to be moved. Findings from this type of evaluation can help a project course-correct early on if it suggests that the intended process is not being adhered to or not working. For example, an annual process evaluation will help identify gaps and fix issues in community engagement, leadership, communications and program implementation before they become issues capable of affecting outcomes.

An **outcome evaluation**, asking the question "did the project successfully move the needle on community issues?" should be done every 2 to 4 years.

Since the intended impact of most community indicators projects is to build knowledge and capacity in the community, assessing and isolating the causal link between community indicators and changes in community conditions poses substantial challenges.[21] Therefore, an outcome evaluation will look as to whether the proper elements are in place to effect change in the community. An outcome evaluation can be helpful in comparing resources and places of change in the community. They could identify a need to shift resources and programming to different areas or people

Any evaluation must be preceded by a period of careful design and deliberation on the key questions to be answered by the evaluation and the methods for answering these questions. In Table 2, we show questions that process and outcome evaluations may ask.

Table 2: Evaluation Questions for Community Indicators Projects - Process and Outcomes

Process => correct steps are taken	Outcomes => community indicators are actionable
✓ Are necessary resources identified and used?	✓ Type of public engagement: Who was engaged and when and to what extent?
✓ Were/are necessary parties at the table?	▪ Community
✓ Is input received and accepted?	▪ Decision makers
✓ Are mechanisms in place to consult experts as needed?	▪ Stakeholders
✓ Are indicator criteria in place?	▪ Funders
✓ Are best practices for data management (e.g., external backup, data planner, data sharing agreements) used?	✓ Do indicators comply with their selection criteria?
	✓ What is the popularity of each indicator (e.g., as indicated by webpage statistics or mentions)?
✓ Is reporting done regularly in a format accessible to target audience(s)?	✓ Have the demographics or other characteristics of the community changed and are the data sufficiently disaggregated to capture those changes?
	✓ Are new information sources available?

- ✓ Are communications tools (e.g., Website, social media, publications) used and tracked?
- ✓ Does the project reach out to the community (e.g., participation in events, public meetings, data days, etc.)
- ✓ Have steps been taken to insure program sustainability?

- ✓ Are there gaps in coverage based on existing or new issues?
- ✓ Are communications effective?
- ✓ What is the maturity level of the indicator project (see Appendix D)?
- ✓ Is an equity filter used in selecting data scale?
- ✓ Are (at least some) indicators actionable?

ACTION

Any community, whatever its current state, aspires to better conditions. The insights provided by indicators about specific community trends and their impacts on overall community conditions are a foundation for change.

As illustrated in Figure 2 (p.11), not every community indicators project will strive to be directly involved in moving the needle. At the very least, the organization will have delivered an actionable report to the community and the indicator development process will have created new connections, partnerships and collaborations that may become the basis for an organized approach to moving the needle on some indicators. It may have served to launch new careers, political and justice agendas, and plant new ideas in community – often referred to as "seeding work." It may have also delivered ammunition for politicians and others to become more active on issues they are sympathetic to.

We are the connectors at the CRC that drives collective action. Because that's really what indicators projects are all about, right? We are formed not just to collect data, but really about analyzing the data of a region, and using the data to drive change.

Jesse Harris
Capital Region Collaborative's
Community Indicators Project [22]

Organizations that initiated the indicator process to provide context to an issue they were already working on will continue working on that issue, but with a better understanding of the context. Often these organizations will take on a more active role in interrelated issues (e.g., a child health organization now involving itself in city planning issues).

However, for projects whose goal is to reach Stage 5 – the process of translating the insights into positive changes for the community – passive approaches, such as including lists of resources, contacts, or promising practices that could be used to move the needle with indicators, are a good first step. Many organizations will opt to start an initiative, often taking on the role of community organizer to help the community prepare itself to improve conditions. This is a big commitment that involves activities to keep the community engaged, organization of committees to take on particular issues, and/or some incentive systems or commitments to support change.

Momentum is growing around the idea that the most effective action is collective –that is, action that is based upon partnerships among different kinds of organizations that agree to join forces in a targeted way around a particular trend, or the need for more information in decision-making more broadly[23].

See Chapter 8 for a more detailed approach to moving from data to action.

Thinking ahead: sustainability challenges

Regrettably, and not unlike the story in other realms of voluntary and community work, many efforts in community indicators are short-lived. They appear on the scene in a burst of enthusiasm, dedication, and skill, experience a hard slog to establish an initial reputation and reporting system, and then struggle to stay relevant or even alive.

Different perspectives exist on the reasons for this boom-bust cycle, and how it might be broken.

Time in and by itself will cause a drain of resources and energy and a buildup of fatigue-inducing habits that have the power to erode the relationships established with the community, funders, decision-makers and other stakeholders.

Many projects, especially those that have been around for a while, struggle to stay relevant. As a result, the project partnership may decide to dissolve but, more likely, it will lead to a decreasing interest in the project which will exacerbate other problems. Strong indicators coupled with good practices in community engagement and communications that support the use of indicators by the community and decision-makers can help ensure relevance.

Volunteer fatigue can affect the vitality of a community indicator project, but good practices related to partnerships and the "care and feeding" of volunteers will also keep them involved.

Projects that are overly associated with one charismatic leader, dependent on a person that holds most of the knowledge and connections, or that are the pet project of an elected official may not survive if that person moves on. Applying good leadership practices and building strong partnerships will prevent this from happening.

The final straw is often decreased or lost funding; this is also the single most difficult problem to solve. When funding goes down, so does the capacity to support a thriving project. Funding is influenced by the health and stability of the lead organization and the diversity of its revenue sources, the level to which the local community, and its funders, understand the value of indicators, and the strength of the partnerships that were established. The project may cut down on its staffing, research and outreach, leading to a decreased interest in the project on the part of funders, creating a downward spiral. Thus, careful understanding of funding considerations, potential sponsors, and resource needs is essential *before* starting a project.

Projects facing threats, such as those described above, may cut down on outreach and engagement to double down on research and analysis, eventually becoming the proverbial "ivory tower," that is, an entity separated from the community and practical realities. This may work for a while as there may be a specialized audience that is receptive to the well-researched product, but it will not be as effective in the community, and eventually the project will lose the connections that allows it to identify what matters to, and therefore what can be done in, a community.

A Cycle of Excellence

 Over the years our project had grown to over 180 indicators. Through [a large community initiative that involved 16,000 voices], residents prioritized issues and highlighted areas that they wanted to see progress in. Through this effort we were able to reduce the number of indicators that we publicly maintain to 50 indicators. We know that those indicators are aligned with the community's vision and it helped us emphasize the relevance of what the trend lines were telling us

Susan Cohn
JCCP[4]

 Innovation has been central to the [Santa Cruz] CAP longevity in order to keep the project useful.

Michelle Luedtke
Applied Survey Research[25]

Projects that stand the test of time are those that stay relevant to the community and their target audience and are willing to innovate.

They are constantly keeping their ears to the ground to understand evolving or changing priorities; they position themselves ahead of the curve regarding new problems; they commit to periodic evaluations; and they have multiple channels of communication with their intended audience.

They know and understand the community and the community knows and understands them. As a result, they periodically review and update their list of indicators. Some projects may go as far as reorganizing their indicators under a new framework[26] that is based on more recent science (e.g., the Social Determinants of Health) or a new focus for the community as a result of a major event (e.g., on sustainability or resilience following a natural disaster). Even criteria should be re-considered to make sure that they are filtering the right kind of indicators. Projects may also reconsider how they disseminate information as they learn more about their audience's preferences or the target audience changes.

Care must be taken to nurture and expand relationships. Each new stage is an opportunity to re-engage, celebrate, deepen and strengthen the connections with existing partners, and create new ones.

CHAPTER 3:
CRITERIA FOR INDICATOR SELECTION

In developing a community indicators project, particular attention must be paid to the data. Establishing – and using -- strong criteria supports quality and consistency.

In addition to particularities related to context and scale, a suite of criteria [27,28,29,30,31,32,33,34,35,36] can be applied for selecting appropriate indicators.

Criteria for selecting indicators should be used as a filter through which indicators should be run before being finalized. Poorly constructed indicators have very little value and could even be dangerous.[37] While some criteria should be a prerequisite for any set of community indicators (e.g., logically or scientifically defensible; meaningful; actionable), others depend on the local needs and preferences of the community and the resources available (e.g., publicly available). The indicator selection process will likely present challenges in balancing feasibility and other desires.

Some criteria are more important to certain community indicator projects than others (e.g., mappability or the need to be applicable in different settings)[38]. Common themes, however, do emerge. We outline several of the key considerations of indicator selection for community indicator projects.

Practical aspects

All indicators should be meaningful and suitable for comparison. A set of indicators should rely heavily on indicators that are outcome-oriented, actionable and timely, although other indicators may be needed to paint a complete picture of the community vision.

> ➢ *Measurable.* The data for the indicator must be attainable. Depending on resources, this could mean that data already exist and can be acquired for little or no cost or that data do not yet exist, but that the project team has the resources to undertake a robust data-collection effort of a measurable construct in a way that reliably and validly captures the construct.
>
> > • *In a representative way.* If initiating the data-collection process, it will be important to ensure that not only can the topic of interest be measured, but that measurements

can be collected from a representative sample of the community (or the entire community, depending on community size). For example, if public schools within the local school district have data on kindergarten readiness, but half of students are in charter schools, the kindergarten readiness data from the public schools may not adequately represent the situation for all children.

➤ *Feasible for project at hand.* This reflects the resources of the project team. If there are those who have extensive data analysis skills, local partners (i.e., departments of health, school districts) who are willing to supply data, funders who can support the collection of new data, then the project can think creatively about their ideal indicators. If the project team is on a shoe-string budget or has limited data skills, the project will likely need to rely on publicly available data. There are many rich sources of publicly available data (see Appendix A for more information).

➤ *Meaningful.* For any indicator project, the first criterion to meet is whether the indicator reflects information that is important to or useful for the community.

- This can be an issue of framing. For example, if a community is interested in climate change, experts might suggest tracking nitrous oxide. However, the general public is likely to be more responsive if that same indicator is called "greenhouse gas," a more commonly understood phrase.

- One additional consideration here is what *sets* of indicators will be useful in telling the bigger story. For example, if a community is looking at infant mortality rates, it might also be useful to look at the proportion of mothers who received prenatal care and prematurity rates.

➤ *Outcome oriented.* Drawing on the language of logic models,[39] indicators could focus on inputs, (e.g., number of clinicians per capita), outputs (e.g., number of people enrolled in health insurance), or outcomes (e.g., number of people with high self-rated health). Measuring inputs and outputs is often appealing because they are comparatively easier to collect and provide useful information for the management of a project. Outcomes, while sometimes more challenging to measure, reflect the conditions or results that the community considers important and may aim to improve. Outcome indicators are key in tracking whether outcomes are or are not being achieved.

Inputs: What resources do you offer: $, # staff, # computers, (e.g., number of clinicians per capita)

Outputs: Who do you reach and what do they do: # of clients, # of classes, partnerships (e.g., number of people enrolled in health insurance

Outcomes: Changes that happened as a result of program or activities (e.g., number of people with high self-rated health)

- Another way of looking at indicators is in term of *upstream* (why did it happen), *downstream* (why it matters) and *status* or *stock* (what is) indicators. For example, one sequence would be land use practices (upstream) affecting acres of agricultural land (what is) affecting availability of food (downstream). This approach helps understand cause and effect and identify where action can be most effective.

Stock (status – what is happening?) indicators are outcome community indicators.

Upstream (cause – why is it happening?) indicators can be input/output or outcome indicators. They support understanding of root causes.

Downstream (effect – why does it matter?) indicators can be input/output or outcome indicators.

➤ *Actionable.* Related to being outcome oriented, an indicator should inform and/or influence policy or funding, alter behavior, and/or increase general understanding in the community in order to improve community wellbeing. The language of *leading* and *lagging* indicators is also used.

- Leading indicators help provide a picture of what the future will be like, thereby providing avenues for action, and should be emphasized as possible. Conversely, while lagging indicators are useful in highlighting issues of concern, they are less useful in helping to envision a roadmap for what the community can do to progress toward its goals. A combination of mostly leading and some lagging indicators can keep communities informed of progress in key areas of concern while inspiring future action.

Leading indicator: precedes an event and helps in its prediction (e.g., access to nutritious food)

Lagging indicator: follows an event and confirms that a pattern (e.g., proportion of people with diabetes) is occurring

➤ *Timely.* Another key – and related – consideration is whether the indicator will provide information that is useful with regard to time. Can the indicator provide an up-to-date snapshot of what is happening in the community, or will the data be too old to be useful (e.g, two year old data on housing to address homelessness during a time of rapidly changing economic conditions)?

➤ *Strengths-based.* In community-based work, it is important to be able to recognize and identify community strengths in addition to the more readily identified challenges.[40] The inclusion of indicators that focus on community assets, even if somewhat non-traditional (e.g., number of block parties) can emphasize the inherent value of communities, particularly those that may not fare well on more traditional metrics, like child poverty. By being able to track these bright spots from the get-go, a project may get more interest from a community who, for example, may otherwise feel tired of constantly being viewed as a regional problem. This is not to say that all indicators need to be positive. Indicators that identify serious issues (e.g., 55% of families with young children are food insecure) are often among the most motivating to a community when it comes to taking action, but it is important to not paint a picture that will unfairly stigmatize a community.

Thinking strategically about indicators: CNYVitals

Indicators that seem promising at first may need to evolve as a project learns. This was the case for Central New York Community Foundation's CNYVitals project. An initial effort to improve adult literacy was rooted in data pulled from the decennial census. After years of working toward improving adult literacy, they saw little movement of the indicator. CNYVitals realized they needed a new approach to track progress since adult literacy is a lagging indicator and the census data they had been using was updated every 10 years and was thus neither sufficiently timely nor sensitive for their needs. Through a logic model exercise, CNYF Vitals decided to track "meso-level" indicators, those leading indicators where progress may eventually move the needle on adult literacy, where data are available in a timely manner, and where the community can have a rapid and visible impact, for example

- Lead in the house
- Families that read to kids
- Kindergarten readiness

"Now we have the confidence to say 'we want to move the needle in that neighborhood' because now we're able to have that middle level data which means we're not just going to be in black box for 5 years of data – we'll have intermediate steps."
-Frank Ridzi, CNYCF[41]

Technical aspects

Every indicator should pass through the filter of these criteria and be reliable, valid, scientifically credible, and sensitive.

> *Reliable and Valid.* Reliability and validity are key considerations in any measurement process. An indicator that is based on reliable and valid data will help ensure that actions based on findings from the indicator project are well-informed.
> - *Validity* refers to the idea that the measurement tool measures what it is intended to be measuring. Does the indicator really relate to what it is intended to track? To what extent can a measure be generalized to a population or setting?
> - *Reliability* refers to the idea that the measurement tool will yield consistent data. R*eliable* can refer to both the instrument that is used to collect data or the data itself. A reliable instrument (e.g., survey) is one that gives consistent answers across time and context, with responses changing only when the topic of interest has in fact changed. The reliability of sampled data (i.e., data that is collected from

a subset of the community that is intended to represent the whole community) is the idea that responses of one sample are approximately the same as a different sample. This is affected by the size of the sample. Thus, the American Community Survey of the U.S. Census can be a rich source of information, but be wary of ACS data for small geographies where a certain sample *may not* reliably represent the whole. This is less of a concern in larger communities.

➢ *Scientifically **and logically** credible.* In addition to the fundamentals of reliability and validity, indicator projects must also ensure that the selected indicators have an established link to the vision or goals that the community has decided to focus on. The Thriving Cities project's Indicator Explorer[42] provides a set of common community indicators, organized by the strength of the academic evidence supporting the indicator. This list is by no means exhaustive, and there are many other possible indicators that a community could select. In that case, an evaluation of the strength of the evidence connecting the indicator to desired outcomes would still need to be conducted.

➢ *Sensitive.* Collected data are at best a *representation* of underlying phenomena happening. A sensitive indicator is one that is sufficiently responsive to changes in the condition of interest as they happen (i.e., it can adequately reflect changes in that underlying phenomenon).

Thinking strategically about indicators: Baltimore Neighborhood Indicators Alliance (BNIA) [43]

In working at a small scale – the neighborhood level – BNIA works with the local government to pull indicators that are meaningful and relevant. For example:

- A review of neighborhood plans revealed a desire for more on-street events, so BNIA did some research and found that street permits are required to close a street for a block party. Thus, permit data can be used as an indicator of community activities in public spaces.
- Instead of just looking at median home price as an indicator of housing, BNIA includes data on whether homes were purchased with a mortgage (i.e., purchased by someone who will live in the home) or with cash (i.e., an investor) because mortgages or cash purchases have different impacts on the neighborhood.
- BNIA has found that population change is a very useful leading indicator. If population in a neighborhood is growing relative to the city, issues are raised around parking, housing instability and rising housing prices, crime, and gentrification. If population is declining, vacant and abandoned properties become an issue, along with illicit behavior and violent crime. Eventually these contracting neighborhoods lose retails, grocers, banks, and schools.
- Studying neighborhoods over time has led to the finding that there is a threshold of the proportion of properties that can be vacant in a healthy neighborhood: no more than 4%. Since that number can be provided for each neighborhood along with a map of the vacant and abandoned houses, this provides a clear point of action for communities to decide where to prioritize rehabilitation or demolition.

Knowing about and getting data like these examples requires the BNIA team to know their city and have their ears to the ground. Staff are encouraged to "be curious about their city" and attend city meetings. They also keep a running "indicator wish list" of information they think would be useful to the community but haven't found a source for – yet.

CHAPTER 4:
INDICATOR DESIGN AND SELECTION

Introduction

Based on community and stakeholder input collected through outreach and engagement, a project will have general ideas about the community's goals or areas of interest. These areas of interest could relate to specific goals or broad domains; either way, the choices will shape the selection of indicators. In some projects, specific indicators (i.e., the specific data points that will be needed to illustrate how the community is doing with regard to their areas of interest) may have already been suggested. If that is the case, there are still many considerations before an indicator is finalized. This chapter will review considerations when selecting or designing indicators and provide an overview of indicator data.

The essence of indicators: providing context

As we have discussed, indicators are more than just data points; they are a representation of trends that places data in context. More often than not, that context is geographic and/or temporal, but it can also be against standards or targets. Thus, a primary criterion for suitable indicators is that they will be able to provide this context.

 The data is in service to something, we're not just collecting numbers, the data all has a story and purpose behind it.

Seema Iyer

BNIA[44]

TEMPORAL CONTEXT

Indicators are commonly tracked over time, typically with an implicit or explicit goal of showing improvements. At the beginning of a project, it may be possible to pull multiple years of historical data for an indicator. This provides some context for how much variability there is in the indicator from year to year, as well as a chance to note any trends that have already been taking place. Then, as the project moves forward, more values will be added as the years pass. Locally-collected data that can be repeatedly collected work well for these types of indicators as do data drawn from the U.S. Census, which, in addition to its decadal counts, offers reliable annual estimates. Regardless of the source, ensure that the data for the indicators have been collected repeatedly and will continue to be collected in the future using the same method or standards if providing temporal context is a project goal.

Thinking ahead to interpretation, remember that many factors can influence what happens to an indicator over time, so if a project is trying to move the needle on an indicator, they will want to be aware of other key events that could affect the indicator data over the observed time period. For example, any community efforts to provide job training and placement in 2008 would have been heavily impacted by the Great Recession.

GEOGRAPHICAL CONTEXT

In addition to, or instead of, tracking a measure over time, data from one community can be compared to another location, thereby illustrating whether the location is better or worse off than other places. Options for comparisons could include neighboring jurisdictions (e.g., a school district comparing itself to neighboring school districts), larger geographies (e.g., a county comparing itself to the state and/or nation), or different communities having the same characteristics (e.g., a mid-size city in a rural setting comparing itself to other mid-size cities in a rural setting elsewhere in the same country). A map usually offers comparisons between areas at a single point in time. Tables or line graphs provide side-to-side visual comparisons of how change happens over time in multiple locations.

Comparability is always difficult and the justification for choosing an area needs to be well-thought-out and documented since the choice will often invite the criticism (usually when local results are worse than in another place) that the areas do not compare well. Be clear and transparent on why those other geographies were chosen and ensure that all localities involved have comparable data and exist under similar demographic, environmental, social and political conditions. Proximity and relatability are often valued over other similarities by policy-makers.

COMPARABILITY TO A STANDARD

Another approach is to compare against a scientifically accepted standard (e.g., the US Environmental Protection Agency standard for lead in drinking water, or, for a set of indicators, the Healthy People 2020 goals[45] or the United Nations' Sustainable Development Goals (SDG)).[46] Even if the institutions sponsoring those standards appear to be reputable and are respected in your field, carefully research and address any biases that may exist among some members of your community or some stakeholders against those potential sources.

TARGET

Although comparing data to a standard or a geography over time is common practice, another consideration is whether or not the condition reflected in the data is acceptable to your stakeholders. A community can set targets and compare data values to its own aspirations. This approach can be difficult to implement for a full set of indicators, but the community and stakeholders will be empowered by the process and the results. For example, many communities now have a "Vision Zero" for traffic safety[47], denoting that no one should die or be severely injured in a traffic accident. In this case, any traffic-related fatality is still a call to action.

Another approach to targets is to draw inspiration from the methods used by standards such as Healthy People 2020. For example, the national HP2020 target is no more than 9.4% of births are born prematurely[48]. However, some communities may have substantially higher or lower initial values. So instead of using the published standard as the target, consider that HP2020 goals often reflect a 10% change in the current condition. So, in a community with 12.8% of births happening prematurely, a goal of 10% reduction (over 10 years, if following the HP2020 model) would create a target of no more than 11.5% of premature births,[1] a more realistic goal for that community.

Scale and Aggregation

Deciding at what scale data will be collected is another important consideration. In this context "scale" means the level at which the data is collected. Think of scale like a zoom lens – a project could look at smaller scales like neighborhoods within a city (like the Baltimore Neighborhood Indicators Alliance[49]) or a larger scale, like entire counties (e.g., ACT Rochester[50]). When considering appropriate scale for the indicators, a project should ask:

- Will reporting only one set of data at the province, county, or watershed scale provide enough information?
- Will the larger scale mask disparities or impacts among different subareas or populations?
- At what scales are decisions or policies made for that area?
- What scale will resonate with community members and help draw them into taking action?
- Are data and resources available to acquire data at smaller scale?

Typically, the smallest geography available is the most useful in diagnosing issues to address.

Availability of data at the level of specificity needed by the community may be the limiting factor. For example, if a community wants to look at each ZIP code or neighborhood separately, not all data can be broken out in such detail. Neighborhood-level data in particular can be difficult to acquire since neighborhoods are not always clearly delineated and do not always match the more readily available data at the ZIP code or census-track levels. Even larger geographies may not always be available. The Behavioral Risk Factor Surveillance System (BRFSS), for

---

[1]Recall the difference between percent and percentage points. To figure out a 10% reduction, take the current value and multiply it by 0.9. That .9 represents the 90% of cases (100% minus the goal of 10% reduction) that will be allowed in the new target. In the example given in the text, 12.8% x 0.9=11.52%.

example, includes an abundance of data on different health-related behaviors but is only readily available at the state level or for a finite set of metropolitan areas.[51]

In addition to this issue around the geographical community, projects should also consider looking at indicators through different lenses that reflect the social and cultural communities. Disaggregating data by sex, income levels, rural/urban residence, or ethnic, racial, or cultural group affiliation can reveal important differences, especially for projects focused on equality or social justice. Many communities, for example, may be interested in seeing whether the educational system is serving all children equally well. In addition to data on the primary indicator, this community would need associated data on race/ethnicity to examine progress among specific groups. Other types of data disaggregation may be very specific to particular indicators.

Logistics: The anatomy of an indicator

An indicator often appears as a simple number. Behind that number though, is a set of additional pieces of information, often termed "metadata." The **metadata** provide keys to interpreting the specific data point as well as connecting it to other data. Key pieces of metadata can include: the title of the indicator, a description or explanation (e.g., among all women giving birth in 2018 in the county, the proportion who self-reported smoking tobacco at any time during their pregnancy), dates available, type, format, source, and geographic coverage. When it comes to source, it helps to be as specific as possible so that subsequent data pulls can be sure to replicate the initial indicator. For example, saying the source is the United States Census is much less useful than saying the source is *Table S0802: Means of Transportation to Work by Selected Characteristics* from the 2012-2016 American Community Survey 5-Year Estimates.

A good practice is to research and include the following information in a metadata file for each indicator[52]:

- Indicator Name
- Indicator definition (see box below)
- Geography
- Source
- Timeliness (how old is the data and how often does it get updated)
- Policy relevance or strength of the research linking this indicator to the goal
- Interpretation: What a high / low level of the indicator value means
- Interpretation: Potential for error due to bias and confounding[2]
- Confidence interval

---

[2] For example, research that associates certain benefits to a physical characteristic of a person, without looking at the fact that a person with those characteristics might also have a different lifestyle.

Metadata and data go hand in hand. Good decisions depend on the most appropriate indicator populated with the best available data. Scrutinizing metadata will help you assess if an indicator is relevant, able to be populated with reliable data, and likely to have a desired effect when communicated well[1].

Making detailed metadata available to users will enhance the communications power of your community indicators.

CHAPTER 5:
DATA ACQUISITION AND DATA SOURCING

This section covers the steps to source, acquire and manage necessary data. Quality data, at the right scale and presented in a manner that facilitates understanding and trust in your community, is necessary to galvanize community action.

Types of data

Data will be collected from two broad categories of sources: primary and secondary.

Primary data are collected by the indicator project staff themselves. Primary data can be collected through surveys, conversations, or observations. Most projects avoid the collection of data because: 1) it can be expensive; 2) it can be time-consuming; and/or 3) it may require the application of standards, knowledge, and practices beyond their capability. The advantage of primary data collection is that it can sometimes provide unique and critical information about a specific area of interest.

Secondary data are collected by someone else. Most community indicator efforts rely heavily on secondary data. Although secondary data is typically easier and more cost-effective to obtain, care must be taken verify the validity, reliability, and the source. Try to obtain the source's metadata or data dictionary. Where proportions are used, make every effort to obtain the numerator and denominator of the variable being summarized. Even large government agencies can make errors, such as miscalculating statistics by using the wrong denominator. If the data includes raw numbers, then it is easy to check the derived values presented.

A SPECIAL CASE OF SECONDARY DATA: ADMINISTRATIVE DATA

Administrative data is information compiled by agencies in the course of administering programs, complying with regulations or meeting contractual requirements. These data reflect day-to-day processes, transactions and record keeping (e.g., school enrollments; hospital admissions; building permits; and vital statistics). These sorts of data are collected systematically. Thus, when compared to surveys, administrative data are often much more complete. Because they are generated by and agency through a program or service, they do not impose a further burden on respondents. Whereas for a survey, there will be people who choose never to start the survey, don't complete the survey, and/or didn't understand the survey questions and answered incorrectly. These issues, known as errors, are minimized with administrative data.

Local governments and agencies can be great sources of administrative data; however, such data are sometimes difficult to obtain. Many governmental agencies, for example, are short-staffed, and constructing a custom data extract may take valuable staff time. Also, the owner of the data may be protective of the information because of privacy concerns and, as a result, be hesitant to share. It is best to approach administrative data relationships in a deliberate fashion, working toward a Data Sharing Agreement.

Potential limitations that users of administrative data need to be aware of include: 1) potential lack of quality control, 2) possibility of having missing items or missing records, 3) changes in the way data is collected over time that make it impossible to compare data from different time periods, 4) differences in concepts which might lead to bias problems, as well as coverage problems, 5) timeliness of the data, and 6) time, resources, skills, and potential cost that may be required to organize and analyze administrative data[53].

Data Acquisition Planner

A data acquisition planner or agenda will support a systematic process for acquiring data. The data acquisition agenda identifies what data is desired, the release dates for specific datasets, if known, and document all of the steps, chronologically, that have been taken to acquire a particular dataset and, such as who took what action on what date, contact information of the person receiving a data request, web sites accessed, etc. Such a document will increase the probability of eventually obtaining the most useful, valid and compelling data.

Data Practices

As data are acquired, a pristine copy should be saved – this unmodified copy will be valuable if the working file gets corrupted or deleted somehow. Appropriate metadata for those data should also be documented and saved alongside the original file. Finally, establish a regular routine for backing up the data, preferably off-site. This will also pay big dividends in the long run.

Data Sharing Agreement

Depending on the source of the data, a formal **data sharing agreement** may be required or should be in place. This is a special form of Memorandum of Understanding (MOU) between the data owner and recipient that should be in place before requesting and sharing data sources and include clear direction for data acquisition and use.

This agreement should include all of the specifics related to data acquisition, including exhaustive metadata, how the data will be protected to prevent proprietary issues, potential unauthorized access, damage, or inappropriate manipulation of the data. Include in the data plan agreement who owns the data after they have been transferred from the source and who has the rights to use and publish the data and any analyses based on the data, how the data will be securely stored. Data confidentiality clauses as its related to access to names or sensitive information by staff or volunteers of the project can also be included.

The agreement should be renewed at regular intervals (e.g., yearly). This process should be recorded in the data acquisition agenda.

Data for community indicators can be obtained from a wide variety of sources, including national, state and local government agencies; academic institutions; foundations, hospitals, nonprofits; libraries; and data intermediaries.

Data Sources

The U.S. Census Bureau through its decennial census and American Community Surveys provide large amounts of data that go well beyond demographic characteristics, covering many other topics such as housing, health, transportation, etc. Governmental departments at the state level may provide easy access to data. For example, the Florida Department of Health maintains FLHealthCHARTS. This portal provides access to a number of datasets, at small levels of geography, related to health, mortality, morbidity, etc. Local government departments can also provide access to data ranging from housing information at the parcel level to voting patterns.

Foundations may have data in-house or have access to data that guides their activities. For example, a large well-funded foundation looking to address health inequities may have deep reach into health organizations that can provide you with data, and with their support, your project may gain access to data aggregated to census tract by local hospitals.

Reaching out to the academic institutions may also produce good results. Many have a centralized data center, staffed by knowledgeable folks who are passionate about using data. For example, the University of Pittsburg maintains a listing of experts by subject area[54].

Nonprofit agencies can provide information about service delivery and concentrations of clients in need. A local nonprofit that does childcare referrals, for example, may have a dataset highlighting access to quality childcare.

Libraries are also excellent partners. Research librarians are highly skilled at tracking down data and potential sources. Many times, library systems or librarians affiliated with universities will have listings of experts by discipline.

Local data intermediaries are groups that connect data and local stakeholders: nonprofits, government agencies, foundations, and residents. These groups work to make data more accessible and useful. They often partner with community indicator projects to provide technical assistance and other resources, such as comprehensive lists of administrative data sources.

For a fee, some data intermediaries and consultants offer custom data sets from large volumes of public and licensed data points. These organizations can also help broker agreements, collect data, maintain data visualization tools, and make the data available to the public.

A comprehensive list of data sources from federal agencies with data available at small geographies (i.e., county level, city, census track, or ZIP code) and other free data access to specialized databases from interest groups are included in Appendix A.

Building Relationships and Connections

While a lot of data can be accessed via portals, fostering relationships with research and planning staff can be key to access better, more specific datasets. One cannot emphasize enough the importance of maintaining healthy relationships with research and planning staff, regardless of where they are found. Take some time to determine who, within an entity, is reliable. Find out who can be counted on to provide you with accurate data in a timely manner. Treat them fairly and reciprocate if they make requests of you – these relationships are very valuable.

Contact the staff that are doing the work in government and data centers. Sometimes, they have relationships with data providers that have taken them years to cultivate and working with them can accelerate data acquisition efforts. Even though the portal did not mention it, a discussion with a person in a county's economic development department may reveal, for example, that they have access to large volumes of data, such as employment and unemployment rates and proprietary datasets that could be use with permission.

Data Gaps

Finding the right data at the right scale with proper temporal coverage is an ongoing challenge for community indicators projects.

Some indicators are so new or innovative that there are no data for that topic. Don't despair; if that indicator is important to the members of your community – and was not rejected when passed through the criteria filters, it deserves to be kept. Options include:

The community really cared about public events and parties. We figured out that every time a block party happened, a permit from the city was needed, so we worked with the city to track the number of permits it granted. It's an important indicator of activity in the public space.

Seema Iyer

BNIA[55]

- Do primary data collection (e.g., a survey or a count). This is the most ambitious approach, and it will require an understanding of some basic field research methods. For a survey, seek guidance on survey construction and sampling techniques. If you do not have the resources to outsource the survey, consider asking appropriate professionals from a local academic institution review the method and questions
- Provide qualitative information and/or interviews that explain or support the indicator, until you are able to obtain quantitative data
- Use a proxy measure. Consider what else relates to the indicator you are researching. Can something else be used instead? For example, the proportion of students eligible for free or reduced-price lunch at school is a common proxy for economic hardship among the student population

To get a picture of the number of businesses by affordability, we work with Yelp to get their data that has the $ sign to get an estimate of business affordability.

Megan Wall

CMT Data Portal[56]

We have addressed the importance of disaggregating data to give a clear picture of how subgroups impact an issue, but what if data for a particular indicator cannot be disaggregated? Inquire with local agencies or nonprofits about any recent surveys that may include relevant data. Consider unfamiliar or nontraditional sources that may be able to support the researchers or the community's hypotheses or instincts. For example, data from a private hospital could augment data from a public health department to provide a more complete picture of how disease incidence and prevalence is impacted by race or ethnicity.

Don't forget to document any steps in your data acquisition agenda.

CHAPTER 6:
DATA LITERACY

Data literacy is necessary to understand, interpret the data and then present it with the right information and caveats so it can be trusted and used. There are a variety of different statistics that community indicator projects will encounter and want to duplicate in their own projects. The following section introduces basic statistics and ways on constructing indicator values. It includes indicators that are constructed from simple arithmetic procedures (e.g., total) as well as indicators that are created from statistical procedures, including those that are more complex and nuanced (e.g., weighted statistics and indices).

Data Types, Formats, and Structures

Data, plural from of the word datum, are pieces of information used for reference or analysis. **Datasets** are collections of similar data.

QUALITATIVE AND QUANTITATIVE DATA

Although indicators are most frequently constructed using quantitative data, indicator projects may oftentimes use qualitative data to enhance interpretation and flesh out the stories about an indicator.

Quantitative data are measures of values or counts reported through numbers. They can tell us how much, how many or how often. For example, the number of residents with access to a vehicle, the number of homeless youths, yearly rainfall, the proportion of mothers receiving adequate prenatal care are all quantitative in nature. Quantitative data from many people or places can quickly be summarized and presented as a single statistic.

Qualitative data, on the other hand, rely largely on words rather than numbers, and are sometimes measures of type. As such, they are not easily summarized. Qualitative information can be essential in providing context to quantitative data points and helping to understand factors that contribute to them. Qualitative data is often collected via individual interviews or focus groups, but it can also be collected in open-ended (i.e., write-in) questions in surveys. The visioning process of an indicators project is filled with qualitative data, and many reports use personal stories to engage their readers.

POPULATION VERSUS SAMPLE

In statistics, a population is any complete group with at least one characteristic in common. Populations may be whole or subgroups of people, animals, businesses, vehicles, events, etc. When examining data, it is important to clearly identify the population being studied or referenced, so that you can understand who or what is included in the data. For example, high school graduation rates may be very different for all 18 year old youth in a city in 2018 versus youth who completed 12th grade in public schools in 2018.

In contrast to an entire population, a sample is a subset of a population. Samples typically aim for being representative; that is, they reflect the characteristics of the entire population. A representative sample lets researchers make inferences about the whole population without the work of collecting data from every single person. Getting a representative sample often includes a methodical plan for who or what will be sampled.

DATA VARIABLES AND MEASUREMENT SCALES

Items of data that vary are oftentimes referred to as **variables**. They are characterized by levels of measurement: **categorical**, describing a quality (e.g., race) or **numeric**, describing a measurable quantity (e.g., income). There are two types or categorical variables: ordinal and nominal. **Nominal** variables cannot be organized in any logical sequence (e.g., eye color, race). **Ordinal** variables, on the other hand, can take on values that can be ordered or ranked (e.g., small, medium, large).

Numeric variables are either interval or ratio. **Interval** variables specify that the distances between each interval on the scale are equivalent. A popular example of this level of measurement is temperature in centigrade. In this measure of temperature, the interval between 40° C and 60° C, for example, is the same as the distance between 100° C and 120° C, but zero doesn't mean no temperature at all. Time is another good example of an interval scale. **Ratio** variables are similar to interval scales but have an absolute zero as well (e.g., distance or weight). Most indicators use interval or ratio scales and present summary values derived from some arithmetic or statistical procedure.

DATA STRUCTURES

Data can be stored using a variety of data structures; however, most often community indicator practitioners will be working with tabular data. Tables contain information presented and stored in cells that are organized in rows (i.e., records) and columns (i.e., fields). The cells hold values that are either numeric (e.g., 123) or string values (that contains text, e.g., abc or abc123). Values held in a numeric format can have all mathematical operations performed on them. However, string variables are limited to few summary operations and are not used in computations. They are generally used to indicate categories or groups. Tables hold the data in the user interfaces typically presented to users in spreadsheets, databases and most statistical packages. These data can be manipulated, summarized and analyzed in readily-available tools like MS Excel (free version available), MS Access, Apple Numbers, and Google Sheets (free).

More complex analyses are best accomplished with specialized statistical programs like SPSS , SAS , Stata , and R (free).

A Special Case of Tabular Data: Spatial Data

Spatial data also known as geographic data, are most often held in individual or collections of tables that hold data linked to location information, called features. **Features** can be points (e.g., schools), lines (e.g., bus routes) or polygons (e.g., school catchment areas, census tracts). The coordinates (i.e., latitude and longitude) are stored and accompany attributes (i.e., characteristics) associated with the features, such as student enrollment at a school (point), length of a bus route (line), or the number of families in a school catchment area (polygon). These data are typically analyzed and visualized in a Geographic Information System (GIS).

Community indicator projects are most often concerned with the creating summary statistics for point data, such as household characteristics or average age for individual residing in some geography of interest (e.g., neighborhood). A process called **geocoding** is used to place geographic coordinates or an address to a place on the earth's surface.

Aggregated and Disaggregated Data

Data can be combined or broken down in many different ways. We introduced the concept of aggregating and disaggregating data earlier but will expand here in the context of scale and privacy. To aggregate data is to compile and summarize data moving from smaller units of analysis to larger. For example, data from individuals on age, race/ethnicity, sex, or income level may be combined into a larger dataset to provide a value that reflects the population as a whole. Most publicly available data received from government sources is in aggregate form. Aggregating data protects the privacy of those involved. Some organizational entities, such as school districts or hospitals only share aggregated data.

To disaggregate data is to break down data into its component parts or smaller groups of data, such as age, race, ethnicity, sex, income level, etc. Data disaggregated by subgroups can show important trends and patterns to help identify where to focus attention.

Care must be used to protect the privacy of individuals when using disaggregated data. Community indicators projects may want to establish data suppression guidelines for this purpose. Data suppression refers to the process of withholding or removing selected information to protect the identities, privacy, and personal information of individuals. Suppression may also be employed to reduce estimates with unacceptable statistical reliability. This practice is regularly used by the U.S. Census Bureau when reporting results for small levels of geography from survey data, such as the American Community Survey.

Data suppression should be used whenever there is chance that the information contained in a publicly available report could be used to reveal or infer the identities of specific individuals. Data partners may already have their own suppression guidelines. These are thresholds for how many people must be represented in order to present a value. For example, if there are 100 children in a local school and three of them are in special education, reporting that either three children or 3% of children in the school are enrolled in special education programs may make it too easy to identify those children. Thus, a district may stipulate that any value below a certain threshold (e.g., less than 25 children or 5% of the school population) not be reported. Indicators for those subgroups may just read as "N/A" in a table for "not available." Do not insert zeroes when data are suppressed or missing, as this will lead to potential errors. Missing data is often indicated with a period in the cell. Conversely, a true '0' is often reportable since there is no one to protect.

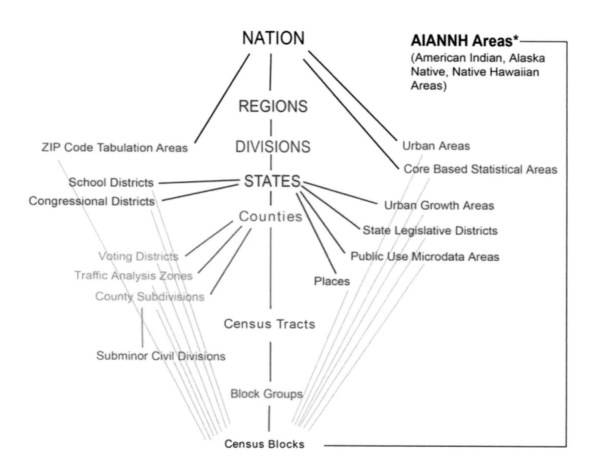

Figure 6: Standard Hierarchy of U.S. Census Bureau Geographic Entities

Spatial data can also be aggregated and disaggregated. Spatial Relationship shows census geographies arranged hierarchically on the vertical spine of the graphic. These geographies are nested and those lower in the hierarchy census (e.g., blocks) can be aggregated to form geographies higher in the hierarchy (e.g., block groups or census tracts). Geographies that are higher in the hierarchy (e.g., counties) can be disaggregated into geographies lower in the hierarchy (e.g., census tracts). Geographies that are not presented on the spine in strict

46

hierarchical order, such as ZIP Code Tabulation Areas (ZCTA), may be hierarchically related to some geographies but they are not necessarily nested. For example, a ZCTA can cross multiple tract boundaries. When using American Community Survey data, you may find that some variables are available at large geographies, like counties, but the same variable is not available at small geographies. This is due to suppression, where small numbers sampled results in unreliable estimates.

Understanding ZCTA and ZIP Codes

For those working with U.S. data, note the difference between ZCTA and ZIP Codes. ZIP stands for Zone Improvement Plan and ZIP codes are used by the U.S. Postal Service to delineate and optimize mail delivery routing. They may not relate to any other administrative, organizational or geographic system of organizing (e.g., town boundaries).

ZCTAs are tabulated every ten years by the U.S. Census Bureau and only roughly approximate ZIP Codes. In the interim years between decennial censuses, the boundaries between ZCTA and ZIP codes may diverge sharply, especially in areas of rapid population growth, where the Postal Service is forced to adjust ZIP codes to accommodate demand.

This presents a conundrum for community indicator practitioners who want to present local data at the ZIP code level. Error is introduced when demographic data from ZCTA is used to augment survey and/or other data captured at the ZIP code level because the geographic boundaries may not overlap. A similar issue arises when ZCTA geospatial files (e.g., U.S. Census Tiger ZCTA) are used to hold data aggregated by ZIP code. ZCTA and ZIP code data need to be handled with an abundance of care in order to present a clear picture to your audience. If a community indicator project desires to present ZIP code data, they should regularly check with the Postal Service to ensure that there have been no changes in boundaries.

Creating neighborhood profiles is practical example of how data from smaller geographies can be aggregated to provide larger custom geographies. For example, many community indicator practitioners aggregate data from smaller Census geographies (e.g., blocks) that fall within neighborhood boundaries to obtain neighborhood demographics and other census information for the neighborhood as a whole.

Interpreting Statistics

Starting at the most basic level, a **sum** is the amount resulting from addition of two or more numbers. The total is the sum of all numbers in a set of numbers. The total population for a neighborhood, for example, is a common indicator, and it is computed by summing the number of individuals in each household in the neighborhood.

Totals are often used in either the **numerator** or **denominator** to compute more complex indicators, such as a population density.

This is calculated by dividing the total population by the land area. For example, if a neighborhood has a total population of 10,000 people and an area of 10 square miles, it would have a population density of 1,000 people per square mile.

$$\text{Population density} = \frac{\text{Numerator} = 10,000 \text{ people}}{\text{Denominator} = 10 \text{ square miles}} = 1,000 \text{ people per square mile}$$

Population density is most useful when comparing small levels of geography, such as neighborhoods or census tracts. Density for subpopulations can also be calculated. For example, an agency providing children's services may use the population density for children under 18 to help identify potential service delivery locations.

Population density is an example of a **ratio**, which is the relationship between one number and another, computed by dividing one number by the other. **Proportions** are ratios where the denominator is the total and numerator represents a part of the total. If, for a given county, the total population was 500,000, comprised of 300,000 females and 200,000 males, the proportion of females in the county would be found by dividing 300,000 by 500,000 to obtain a dividend of 0.6. Thus, we could say the proportion of females in the country is 0.6. To translate this into a percentage, one would multiply the proportion by 100 to obtain 60%.

$$\text{Proportion of females in County} = \frac{\text{Numerator} = 300,000 \text{ females}}{\text{Denominator} = 500,000 \text{ inhabitants}} = .6 \times 100 = 60\%$$

Rates refer to the occurrence of a specific event over time, usually expressed in relation to a well-defined constant, such as 100, 10,000 or 100,000. Graduation rates and rates of chronic diseases are frequently encountered. Graduation rates are typically calculated by dividing the number of students who graduate in four years with a regular high school diploma by the number of students who form the adjusted cohort for the graduating class. The a simply considers the number of students entering and leaving the cohort of students who started ninth grade together. Graduation rates are expressed as rate per 100. The graduation rate for subgroups, such as race or gender, are used to highlight inequities and areas in need of improvement. For example, the Florida graduation rate for school year 2016-17 for White females was 89.4%, but the graduation rate for White males was 83.1 %, a difference of 6.3 percentage points. Qualitative data that attempts to explain these differences would be of interest to educators, advocates and policy makers. Community indicators projects may want to look at a given rate in their locale and compare against state or national rates as benchmarks.

Chronic disease rates highlight the importance of specificity when presenting indicators. There are a number of chronic disease rates to consider; two examples being incidence and prevalence. **Incidence** is the number of newly diagnosed cases of a disease in a specific time period. An incidence rate is the number of new cases of a disease divided by the number of persons at risk for the disease. If, over the course of one year, five women are diagnosed with breast cancer out of a population of 200, the incidence of breast cancer in this population would be 0.025 cases per year. This could be generalized to a rate of 2,500 per 100,000. Note that birth and death rates are often reported as rates per 1,000. **Prevalence** is the total number of cases of a disease existing in a population divided by the total population. For example, if in a city of 40,000 people, 1,200 were recently diagnosed with cancer (i.e., incidence) and 3,500 were living with cancer, then the prevalence of cancer is 0.118 (4,700/40,000), or 11,750 per 100,000 persons.

The above example are **crude** rates of disease. However, many times rates are adjusted to remove the effect of a variable, such as age or sex, to permit unbiased comparison between groups or geographies. Imagine comparing the death rate in a county with a very elderly population to a county with a large millennial population. The crude rate would likely indicate a higher death rate among the county with the large elderly population. By adjusting the calculation for differences in age, you can make the county comparisons seem a bit more apples-to-apples. Age adjusted rates are helpful in comparing place (e.g., health facilities or catchment areas) where the incidence and/or prevalence are impacted by age.

The table below demonstrates how these rates are calculated. The six columns show fields containing age group, number of deaths (a), actual size of the total population in millions (b), rate per 100,000 (c=a/b*100,000), weight (d), and weighted rate (c*d) with values for the different age groups. Rate per 100,000 shows Age-Specific Rates, and the crude morality rate for the total population (229.8) is shown in red. The Weight in the fifth column is the proportion of the U.S. population for each age group, adding up 1. This proportion is multiplied by the Age-Specific Rate to get the Weighted Rate. These are then summed to get an Age-Adjusted Rate for the U.S. Population, which is shown in red (i.e., 214.7 per 100,000).

Table 3: Age Age-Adjusted Mortality Rate for Cancer in US (U.S. Census Bureau)

Age Group	Number of Deaths (a)	Population in Millions (b)	Rate per 100,000 (c=a/b*100,000)	Weight (d)	Weighted Rate (c*d)
Birth-14	62	1.95	3.2	0.284	0.91
15-24	82	1.21	6.8	0.174	1.18
25-34	303	1.48	20.9	0.123	2.57
35-44	686	1.40	40.9	0.113	5.54
45-54	1,630	1.02	159.8	0.114	18.22
55-64	3,457	0.73	475.0	0.091	43.31
65-74	6,352	0.58	1093.4	0.061	66.70
75-84	5,443	0.29	1878.3	0.030	56.35
85+	2,050	0.07	2841.5	0.007	19.89
Total	20,065	8.73	229.8	1.000	214.7

Use the different types of rates to appropriately support the intent of an indicator. Age-adjusted rates of diabetes for example may be appropriate for comparing different counties, while crude rates will better illustrate the need for diabetes-related action or resources.

Another example of weighting is used when calculating inflation adjusted dollars, which equates the buying power of dollar values collected temporally (e.g., years) by weighting values (e.g., median salary) using the Consumer Price Index (CPI). The CPI is a measure of the average change over time in the prices paid by urban consumers for a specific collection of consumer goods and services.

When calculating inflation adjusted figures, one can either 1) state the series in terms of most recent year's dollars or 2) use the beginning year of the series as the reference point. The U.S. Bureau of the Census uses the first approach to present and compare median income figures for the past several years. The second approach is useful in determining if wages are keeping pace with inflation.

Summary Statistics

Summary statistics are used to provide a quick and simple description of a sample data. They include central tendency (i.e., a single value that describes and entire set of data), dispersion (i.e., describes variability in the data), shape of a distribution and dependence (dependence of two statistics). Two measures of central tendency are the mean and median of a sample. The **mean**, also known as the average, is the sum of all the values divided by the observations or records. The **median** is the value that falls in the middle of a set of sequentially-ordered data.

For example, if a hospital had 7 nurses who have worked for 2, 5, 5, 11, 12, 15, and 21 years, respectively, the mean length of tenure would be 10.1 years, while the median length of tenure is 11 years. An unexpected or unusual value, also known as an outlier (i.e., extraordinarily high or low value at either or both ends of the distribution), can dramatically affect the mean. If 21 was replaced by 48, the average tenure would increase to 14 years. In this case, we may call 48 an outlier. The median is less sensitive to skewed distribution, so if 21 was replaced by 48, the median would still be 11, which is more reflective of the tenure for nurses in our hypothetical sample.

Length of service of 7 nurses in a hospital: 2, 5, 5, 11, 12, 15, 21		
Mean or average	(2+5+5+11+12+15+21)/7	10.1 years
Mean with outlier	(2+5+5+11+12+15+48)/7	14 years
Median	2 – 5 – 5 – 11 – 12 – 15 - 21	11 years
Median with outlier	2 – 5 – 5 – 11 – 12 – 15 - 48	11 years

As illustrated, the mean and median can produce very different results, depending on the data set. When analyzing data, thoughtful choices need to be made about which statistic is most appropriate. It is common for community indicators of economic wellbeing, for example, to report the median household income rather than mean household income. This is because households with extremely high incomes pull the average up and this distorts the estimate of the amount of money to which most households have access.

VARIABILITY

When we summarize many values with one statistic, as we do with a mean, it's also important to consider the variability within the set of data. This helps use to assess how accurately the statistic is summarizes the data. The simplest measure of variability to understand is the **range**, which is the difference between the highest and lowest value in a data set. For our data set, 2,5,5,11,12,15, 21, the range is equal to 21 (highest value) minus 2 (lowest value), or 19.

A more informative method of describing variability is with the standard deviation. The **standard deviation** is the square root of the sum of the squared deviations from the mean (i.e., differences from the mean). Looking at the example data set of 2,5,5,11,12,15, and 21, with a mean of 10, we see that three values (2, 5, 5) are pretty far below the mean, two values (11, 12) are slightly above the mean, and two values (15, 21) are far above the mean. A small standard deviation indicates that values cluster around the mean. For our data set, 2,5,5,11,12,15, 21, the standard deviation is 6.6, which could be interpreted a moderate variability among the numbers compared to the mean of 10.1.

The following figure shows two datasets with the exact same mean, but a different standard deviation. Dataset 1 is the nurses's length of employment data used above. Dataset 2 could be length of employment from a different population of nurses, that shows employment length ranging from 7 to 15 years, a spread that that is closer to the average, as shown by the smaller standard deviation.

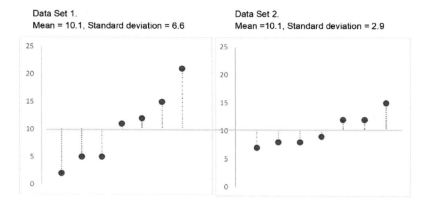

Data Set 1.
Mean = 10.1, Standard deviation = 6.6

Data Set 2.
Mean =10.1, Standard deviation = 2.9

Figure 7: Vertical lines show different variability patterns around the same mean (horizontal line), which result in different standard deviations

Sample Surveys

A **census** counts every unit of a population. For example, every ten years, the U.S. Census Bureau leads an effort to do a complete enumeration. That is, they try to collect data from every single person that makes up the U.S. population[57]. In contrast, **sample surveys** rely on a representative sample to estimate characteristics in the population. Between the decennial census, the Census Bureau collects data from about 3.5 million households via the American Community Survey (ACS) [58]. Statistical techniques are then used to take the information from the sample and estimate the value for the whole population.

SAMPLE CONFIDENCE

Whenever sample data are used, the values collected represent estimates of the "true" population values. The larger the sample size in relation to the size of the population, the more likely that the sample accurately represents the population.

Regardless of the sample size, any value that comes from a survey needs to include information about how much confidence there is that the estimate accurately represents the entire population. One way of describing how good an estimate is by employing a **confidence interval**. A confidence interval consists of three pieces of information: 1) a lower bound, 2) an upper bound and 3) a probability estimate.

The Census Bureau typically reports 90% confidence intervals for all of their estimates, such as from the American Community Survey[59] . The 90% indicates a level of uncertainty about how well the current estimate reflects the actual "true" value for the population. A 90% confidence interval means that if other samples were taken (using the same approach and sample size, but with different people), the true value would lie within the confidence interval 9 times out of 10, or 90% of the time, the confidence interval would contain the true value.

Subject	Honolulu County, Hawaii			
	Estimate	Margin of Error	Percent	Percent Margin of Error
Native Hawaiian and Other Pacific Islander	92,920	+/-1,691	9.4%	+/-0.2
Native Hawaiian	51,008	+/-1,895	5.2%	+/-0.2
Guamanian or Chamorro	2,635	+/-689	0.3%	+/-0.1
Samoan	14,093	+/-1,583	1.4%	+/-0.2
Other Pacific Islander	25,184	+/-1,735	2.6%	+/-0.2
Some other race	8,448	+/-788	0.9%	+/-0.1

Table 4: Example of 2012-2016 American Community Survey 5-Year Estimates data

The confidence interval is related to the **margin of error**, which is defined as the difference between the estimate and the value in the confidence interval. In Table 4, as an example, are few lines from the 2012-2016 American Community Survey 5-Year Estimates for Honolulu County[60]. The table shows the point estimates and margins of error. The Estimate column shows how many people are estimated to be in that category. The Margin of Error column shows the value that should be added or subtracted to the estimate to produce the 90% range. For example, the ACS estimates that there are 14,093 Samoans in Honolulu, but it could actually be as few as 12,510 (14,093-1,583) or as many as 15,676 (14,093+1,583). The Percent column indicates the proportion of the total population (i.e., about 1.4% of people in Honolulu are Samoan). The Percent Margin of Error column extends that percent estimate; that is, the true value could be as low as 1.2% or as high as 1.6%.

It is important to look at the margin of error in relation to the estimate. The larger the margin of error is relative to the estimate, the less reliable the estimate and the more caution should be used when making inferences or deciding on action based on the estimate. In the above table, the margins of error for Native Hawaiian and Other Pacific Islanders are similar in size (1,895 and 1,735, respectively). However, there appears to be about twice as many Native Hawaiians (51,008) as there are other Pacific Islanders (25,184), which indicates that the estimate of Other Pacific Islander is less reliable. Generally, the smaller the subgroup, the less reliable the estimates are.

COMPARING CENSUS AND ACS DATA

Data produced by the U.S. Census Bureau are widely used in community indicators projects and there are a variety of tools, such as American Fact Finder, that make data extraction easy. However, there are some caveats to consider when comparing these data. ACS data are collected yearly and compiled into 1-, 3- and 5-year estimates. A sophisticated sampling methodology is designed to increase confidence in estimates for smaller subgroups and geographies. As a result, ACS estimates can be compared to estimates from the decennial Census and to non-overlapping ACS temporal ranges. For example, the 2013 ACS 1-year estimates can be compared to the 2010 Census, 2015 ACS 1-year estimates, and 2016 3-year estimate. However, the 2013 ACS 1-year estimates cannot be compared to the 2014 ACS 4-year estimate because that estimate includes data from 2013.

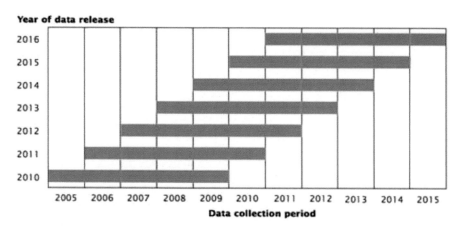

Figure 8: Example of 2012-2016 American Community Survey 5-Year Estimates data

Analysis and Interpretation

Once verifiably accurate data have been acquired and properly computed and laid out, with all data limitations understood and addressed, data can now be analyzed and interpreted.

TRENDS

A **trendline** is a best-fit line based on historical data (i.e., data collected over time and leading to a point as close to present date as possible) that indicates the general direction of a sequence data points plotted over time. This historical information will give some important baseline information about the conditions for an indicator. Most statistical programs, including Excel, will create a scatter plot, based on a dataset, and can add a trendline. The trendline will help visualize whether numbers are going up or down, or have been stagnating. This can then be translated into the various icons (e.g., arrows, stoplights, colors) that a community indicators project can use in a scorecard to show at a glance how well a community is doing on some of those trends.

CORRELATION

Correlations tell us the degree of linear association between two variables. A **scatter plot** lays out a series of points that show the relationship between two sets of data. A correlation coefficient provides the direction and strength of association between the variables. The correlation coefficient ranges from -1 to +1, with a correlation of zero (0.0) indicating no

54

relationship. When two variables are positively correlated (i.e., + sign), as one variable increases the other increases. When two variables are negatively correlated (i.e., - sign), as one variable increases the other variable decreases. In Figure 9, (a) shows a perfect positive correlation; (b) a low negative correlation; (c) a high positive correlation and (d) a very weak positive correlation.

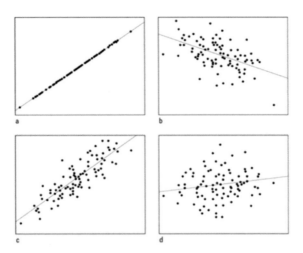

Figure 9: Examples of scatterplots showing different degres of correlation

This statistic is used by communities to demonstrate the relationship between two indicators. For example, income is associated with many community indicators, such as educational attainment. As educational attainment rises, so should income levels. Thus, this is a positive correlation. Income is also a social determinant of health, and rates for many health conditions go up as income goes down. This is an example of negative correlation.

Even though there may be a near perfect correlation between two variables, it does not mean that one variable is causing the variation in the other. Causation can only be implied from true experiments. However, one may infer a causal relationship if there is:

- Temporal precedence - one variable always happens before the other
- Covariation of the cause and effect - the variables are always found together, producing the same observable relationships
- There are no other plausible explanations for the relationship

FORECASTING

Extrapolation is finding a value outside a dataset.

Trend extrapolation is to locate a trend that is apparent over time, and project it forward. This can be a matter of extending a trend line or exponential curve (e.g. economic growth, power or diffusion of a technology) in the future. Extrapolation, of course, can give misleading results because it is "uncharted territory." An economy that has grown consistently for a decade at an average rate of growth of 3% can suddenly crash or a new technology can suddenly stop or reverse the need for a particular source of energy. Limits to growth or decline will often be encountered. For example, a population may not expand beyond a certain carrying capacity, a concept may not diffuse beyond the reach of a technology or cultural practice, and most things will not decline below zero.

Extrapolation can be used to project improvements in community conditions expected as a result of some action, what is also called Turning the Curve in Result Based Accountability[TM]. Correlating lead in paint on house walls with impact on children's cognitive abilities may lead to a community indicators project working with the community and experts to project that for every thousands of dollars invested in lead removal in homes there will be a certain percent increase in future numbers of 3rd grade children reading at grade level.

STATISTICAL PROCESS CONTROL

For community indicators projects, considering the mean along with the standard deviation can help reveal a need to further investigate or support subpopulations at either end of the distribution (i.e., those with very high or very low numbers).

One method is called **Statistical Process Control**[61]. This technique is borrowed from production quality control but is adaptable to community indicator analyses as well. Using this method will result in one of three potential relationships between the mean and the standard deviation:

1. If the mean is at a level the community finds acceptable, and the standard deviation is low, then the indicator suggests everything is good.
2. If the mean is at a level the community finds acceptable, but the standard deviation is high, there may be a need to identify and provide additional support to outliers (i.e., specific individual units with unusual values on the indicator, whether they are hospitals, creeks, or people).
3. If the mean is at a level that the community does not find acceptable, regardless of the standard deviation, then it is likely that the whole system needs attention, rather than just a few outliers. However, it may be that certain groups are driving the mean, so it can still be worthwhile to look at subgroups.

Conclusion

There is nothing more important for a community indicators project than using quality data and presenting it in a way that can be understood and trusted. Finding the right data at the right scale is the first part of the challenge. The sources listed in Appendix A offer troves of datasets to populate just about any common indicator, although not always at the desired scale. Being able to interpret the data and then present it with the right caveats and information is the other side of the challenge. Guidelines on presentation are provided in the next chapter, but, regardless of how the indicators will be displayed, any potential limits on the data's accuracy need to be made evident.

CHAPTER 7: REPORTING

Introduction

Reporting is the process of conveying data to people who may not have it yet. Reporting is a form of dissemination.

The elements of quality reporting are straightforward, but it takes time and skill to bring them together. The most effective indicators projects see reporting as a mix of research, audience analysis, communications, emotion, and design.

While many roles apply to people who use indicators, in this guide they are called users or audience.

As a report is being developed, consider how it relates to the project's communications. A communications plan can be developed for each report, and the report-level plans can be integrated into the project's overall communications strategy. For more, see the Communications chapter (Chapter 10).

> *How do we invest in systems now to be able to keep up with the technology of the future? These are strategic questions a leader has to consider, or else risk not continuing to have a value-add for the local region.*
>
> *Paul Mattessich*
> *Wilder Research[62]*

Goals of reporting

Success for indicators projects means changing minds and influencing behavior.

Therefore, indicators projects should spend a large amount of time considering how indicators and analysis will be used.

The exact form this takes depends on the purpose of each indicators project (see Figure 2 in Chapter 2).

Reporting can serve multiple goals. A report is likely to prioritize one or two goals more than others. For projects that aim to support action indirectly (Level 4) or directly (Level 5 in Fig. 2), effective reporting is particularly important. In addition, some projects will advocate for a position on political or social issues, while others aim to be as neutral as possible. Many projects also build data literacy among users, so users are equipped to do their own analyses.

Here are a few examples of the goals reporting can serve, all of which should contribute to the broader goals above.

INFORMATION

A report that seeks only to inform will include the bare necessities: data points, trends, citations, and context in the form of other data. This report leaves much of the interpretation and further investigation to the users.

Informative reports are simple, replicable, and straightforward. Software can make collection and publication very easy. Some projects use automated technology to pull data directly from online sources, changing the role of human researchers. Even when reports are put together by hand, it can be as simple as plugging an updated number into a template.

There are drawbacks to providing numbers without historic context or details about the effect of structural forces, those societal norms, attitudes or culture that influence us all. For example, there is a difference between unemployment seen as the result of people not having job skills and unemployment caused by ongoing discrimination on the part of employers.

Even in its simplest form, a community indicators report must provide a clear definition of the indicator, what the units of measurement are, the data sources, and any relevant data, or statistical, information.

ANALYSIS

Analysis goes beyond showing data points to explaining what a given indicator means. To analyze data is to scrutinize, synthesize, evaluate, transform, and/or model data to discover useful information, suggest conclusions, and support decision-making.

Data points are often synthesized and evaluated in context with broader trends, including data sets for other geographies or from another time period, while looking for patterns behind trends.

Skillful analysis requires an objective lens. Analysts must be open to data stories that do not fit their expectations.

Analyses must be reported cautiously, taking care to explain the data and the process to lend credibility to the conclusions, while focusing on the story around the conclusions.

ADVOCACY

Whether we recognize it or not, biases shape the whole process of domain and indicators selection. A community interest in children's wellbeing will select different indicators than one mostly concerned over the health of the planet, although good indicator projects starting from either of those angles would still recognize the systemic nature of those priorities and would end up with a lot of overlap. A community indicators project should reflect the reality that communities are complex, interconnected systems.

Indicators can really provide a simplified view of a problem, trend or quality-of-life issue. Understanding the problem and the solution can require more sources of data, like qualitative analysis and digging into the research literature. The solutions themselves can be complex. Weaving the pieces together is one way we should be pushing ourselves as a project.

Allison Liuzzi
Minnesota Compass[63]

Building a community indicators project around an issue and using the report to advocate for a particular issue is appropriate as long as the author's perspective is clear. Reports such as the Annie E. Casey Foundation's Kids Count[64] clearly do that.

Indicators can be chosen to support a community priority, but only to a point. An organization intent on demonstrating that more money needs to be spent on its children can highlight some depressing indicators on a report to the funders but needs to include indicators showing positive as well as negative trends in its report. Many projects report that they find it helpful to combine quantitative and qualitative data in their reports. Personal stories (qualitative data) can help build the audience's connection with the data, which is important in advocacy work.

Our website is a hub for 145 nonprofit partners who provide us with outcome documents that show how their programs or efforts align with [any of] the 59 indicators. We provide microsites to each partner, to show who they are, but also to provide a space for them to talk about their connection to the SA2020 community vision. We point people – individuals who might be on our website -- to either volunteer, or get more information, or even donate to those organizations.

Molly Fox
SA2020[65]

Data should never be manipulated to support a position. It is never appropriate to cherry-pick data points or manipulate timelines in order to try to make a point. The discovery of just one such manipulation would invalidate the trust in the whole effort – and in the organization as a whole. Criteria and best practices decided in advance should hold through the whole reporting process, whatever the results may show.

DATA LITERACY

Many indicators projects have taken it upon themselves to educate the community about data. While many do so through interaction with community members, others use the reporting process and include sections or infographics on the value of data or to explain statistical processes. At the very least, indicators projects should explain and display confidence intervals around the data they use as well as some explanation on the sampling process.

CONNECTIONS

Community indicators provide more than information. Indicators, and the process of developing them, can provide a space for people and organizations to unite around a common cause and develop shared language, values, and goals. A report can offer physical space for connections by providing profiles of community members, highlighting the work of individuals and organizations, or creating opportunities for the exchange of ideas and connections via blog posts or social media.

DATA TO ACTION

Regardless of, or as a complement to, a project's involvement in initiatives to move from data to action, the report itself can include various paths to move from data to action. Many indicators projects include resources such as links or organization contact information that will provide a way for the user to take action to move the needle. Others work with users to build action plans and develop targets, including the information in the report and sometimes organizing the indicators around it. Others may include pledge forms for individuals or organizations to commit to some action to help move the needle. If they are involved in an initiative, the report can include a report on the progress of that work and a call to action.

Reporting formats

There are many different ways to report data. To choose, first make sure you know your audience. Your reporting method should provide information want to know, in a form that will be easy for them to use.

Before choosing a format, think about where and how the data will be published – that may influence its form. Consider the cost for creating and sustaining a reporting vehicle. For example, the cost to print a paper report will depending on its size, color needs, format, and number of copies, while creating a webpage may require setting up a website, paying a designer, and paying ongoing hosting costs. Many formats can be produced in a pure digital or non-digital format. Some can be shared digitally even if they are produced live or in a hard form (e.g., a video of a presentation posted to a website). Projects that use paper formats often still make a file of the report available online.

I don't think new is necessarily better when it comes to reporting. It's about keeping the data updated and using the right thing where needed.

Ann Johnson
ACT Rochester[66]

Some reporting formats are more common than others and lend themselves to the comprehensive reporting of a full set of indicators (e.g., an online dashboard) while others are useful to report on a few indicators, to focus on some areas, or as alternative format to a more traditional format (e.g., a postcard).

Projects can modify formats to fit different audiences, budgets and skill levels. For example, one project may print out reports and place them on local legislators' desks. Another project found that people do not keep printed reports, and has shifted to purely digital distribution.[67] An online report may reach a wider audience, but the costs of maintaining a website can be significant.

Here is a list of formats that indicators projects have used:

- ☐ Article
- ☐ Billboard
- ☐ Blog post
- ☐ Charts and graphs
- ☐ Dance
- ☐ Dashboard
- ☐ Digital interactive
- ☐ Editorial
- ☐ Handheld interactive (e.g., postcard, interactive paper product)
- ☐ Improv

- ☐ Maps
- ☐ Marketing and advertisements
- ☐ Microsite (standalone website)
- ☐ Music
- ☐ Newsletter
- ☐ Podcast
- ☐ Presentation
- ☐ Press release
- ☐ Short-form report (e.g., brief, executive summary, handout)
- ☐ Social media post

- ☐ Infographic
- ☐ Interview
- ☐ Landing page on a website
- ☐ Long form report
- ☐ Text message
- ☐ Theatre
- ☐ Video
- ☐ Webinar

Case study: Minnesota Compass[68]

Minnesota Compass provides a mix of analysis with tables, graphs, and maps with quantitative indicators.

VISUAL REPORTING

Compass provides dozens of Key Measures across topic areas such as Arts & Culture and Education. The indicators are provided with minimal initial context. The goal is to provide a quick takeaway and pique curiosity among users. The tables, graphs, and maps are labeled consistently across the site with a title, description of the geography, time period of the data, and information about the groups represented in the visualization.

Users seeking greater depth can use the "Data & Notes" view to see a broader time period and detailed information for many data sets. Each visualization also includes a link to the source so users can explore on their own.

CUSTOM VIEWS

The Compass website provides data by geographic area as well as topic area. Geographic profiles range from statewide to customizable neighborhood profiles for select areas. To aid in making connections and ensure users draw on comparable data, the team strives to use consistent sourcing and breakdowns between the topical and geographic indicators.

Along with data points, Compass provides both at-a-glance and in-depth analysis of trends. Social media and website features highlight quick takeaways and new data. Meanwhile, Insights Articles provide a space for researchers and community leaders to synthesize data stories and draw meaning from the indicators.

ONLINE REPORTING

Most indicator projects have moved to some sort of online reporting, commonly using dashboards and scorecards to report indicators. These methods synthesize data in a visual form that is easy to digest and readily understandable. One limitation of online reporting, especially in projects that cover large geographic areas, is that community members in rural areas may have limited access to high speed internet access. A map-filled, dynamic, interactive dashboard can offer a lot; however, in places with low speed connections or no internet at all, important constituents may be unable to access the information.

Dashboards and scorecards

Dashboards originally described the display of information in a vehicle. The dashboard provides indicators of a car health and effectiveness: speed, fuel level, engine status, etc. The driver uses that information to operate and maintain the car, travel safely, and, most importantly, reach destinations. Dashboards convey data in real time.

In the context of community indicators and due to the nature of data used to populate indicators, the dashboard is likely to be a time-sensitive, graphical summary of various pieces of important information on the health of a community and the effectiveness of efforts to build on its strengths will be at least time-sensitive.

Traditionally, scorecards display data to track how a community fares (scores) against a target, strategy, or goal.

Among today's community indicators projects, the terms dashboards and scorecards are sometimes used interchangeably in part because both of their distinctive characteristics, timeliness and scoring, are inherent to the concept of community indicators.

Community Indicators in Action

The Baltimore Neighborhood Indicators Alliance (BNIA) has produced its annual Vital Signs scorecard for fifteen years, growing from 100 to 125 indicators each year. Along with the printed version, Vital Signs now includes an online interactive portal with mapping and data visualization. BNIA says, "Vital Signs is getting more valuable over time because now you can see long-term trends in the neighborhoods." BNIA also integrates other reporting channels into its work. "When the Vital Signs report comes out, we also prepare the State of the Neighborhoods presentation. It's ready to go so, no matter the organization, we can offer it to them as a service."[69]

What distinguishes dashboards and scorecards is that they are first designed to be read at a glance. They use icons or other graphic symbols, like thumbs up/thumbs down, or smiley/frowning faces and green-yellow-red color schemes, to convey information (Figure 10). The choice of the green/yellow/red color set associated with the icon design is strongly associated in the subconscious with good/so-so/bad and adds to the intuitive understanding of the meaning of the icons. Consider how well icons can be differentiated upon quick scanning.

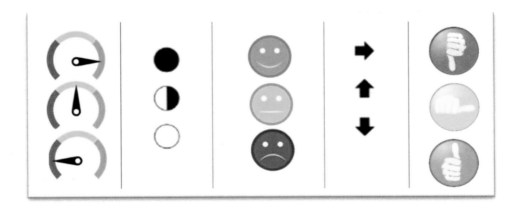

Figure 10: Icons commonly used in dashboards and scorecards to convey such concepts as improving or worsening trends, better or worse than X, target reached or not, etc.

Dashboards and scorecards have multiple layers that offer the options to dig deeper into definitions, analyses, maps, methodology, data sources and other pertinent information.

Figure 11: Coastal Georgia Indicators Coalition's dashboard uses gauges, arrows, color, words, and numbers to compare the value of an indicator with larger geographies (the state and the country), convey the direction of the trend, compare the value for the current year's indicator to previous year's and to the state, and set it against a target [70]

In addition, many dashboards allow for some degree of interaction with options to select certain features, such as comparing several indicators on one graph, or selecting the geographies to which the community could be compared.

Maps

Maps can be used to convey information as part of a dashboard, profiles, or on their own. Like dashboards, maps synthesize data in a visual form that is easy to digest and readily understandable (Figure 12).

Choose a map format that fits how the map is published. For example, if the map will be printed in black and white, choose a simple look and be sure to test a black and white printout. A map used for a public awareness campaign could be more stylized and less accurate, but a map used in public policy planning will likely need a high level of accuracy.

If the map will be published mainly on a website, consider whether or not it will be interactive. Costs can rise quickly for projects creating interactive maps. However, there can also be great benefits. There are some free tools, like Tableau Public,[71] that enable the creation of online visualizations, including simple maps. Interactive maps help users find the information they want in a visual form. Some maps allow users to compare data over time or for different geographic areas. Once the project has an infrastructure in place, the process of updating the data can be quick and efficient.

Test the site on different devices to see how the map looks. Use colors that work well together: there should be enough contrast to tell different colors apart, and some color associations should be avoided (e.g., avoid blue for a map that also includes blue lakes).

Regardless of the format, all maps should be clear and accessible. Take care in designing the labels, colors, and sizes for each part of the map. The legend should be divided into segments that aid understanding. For example, if the data set only includes indicators between 5 and 15 percent, it would not make sense to include a segment called "30% to 40%."

Similar to dashboards, some maps use symbols to show differences between geographic areas or differences over time.

Projects that do quite a bit of mapping may find it helpful to hire a specialist in GIS (Geographic Information Systems). A GIS specialist designs maps using georeferenced spatial data – that is, data points tied to specific locations.

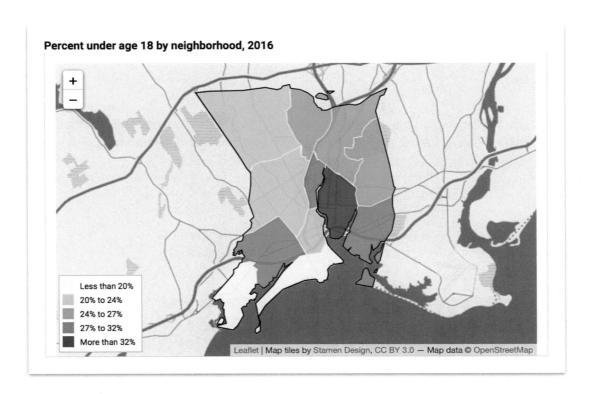

Percent under age 18 by neighborhood, 2016

Less than 20%
20% to 24%
24% to 27%
27% to 32%
More than 32%

Leaflet | Map tiles by Stamen Design, CC BY 3.0 — Map data © OpenStreetMap

Figure 12: Baltimore Neighborhood Indicators Alliance provides interactive maps on its website. The maps use shades of blue and green to show demographic and quality of life indicators. In this example, the title, date, and legend are clearly visible. The focus area is well-defined through the use of color. The rest of the map is included for context. The bottom right corner of the image includes information on how the map was created.

PRINTED REPORTS

Printed reports take a variety of forms. As with other formats, consider what will be interesting and useful for users. Projects must also balance factors like cost and capacity when creating printed reports. Printing costs add up quickly.

Printed reports can be shared many ways. Some projects make reports available online and invite users to print them. Others physically place reports on the desks of stakeholders. Still others distribute printed reports at events.

Here are some common printed formats:

Annual report

Many projects find it useful to create an annual (or bi-annual or tri-annual) report. The annual report can provide a valuable benchmark for the project, its collaborators, and community members. As projects produce a report at regular intervals, community members may begin to look forward to it. Some projects hold an event when they release a report, while others simple notify users about the new data.

Annual reports may include a mix of visualization and analysis. Maps and charts are common. The report may include analysis and a data literacy section for readers to take from the data.

Infographic

A printed infographic can be a good way to get data into peoples' hands. This format combines a lot of information using graphic representations in a stylized, well-designed format to enhance understanding. There are several free tools for creating infographics.

Scorecards

As described above, scorecards and dashboards provide indicators in an easy-to-digest format. Scorecards give a high-level look at the status of a community or issue.

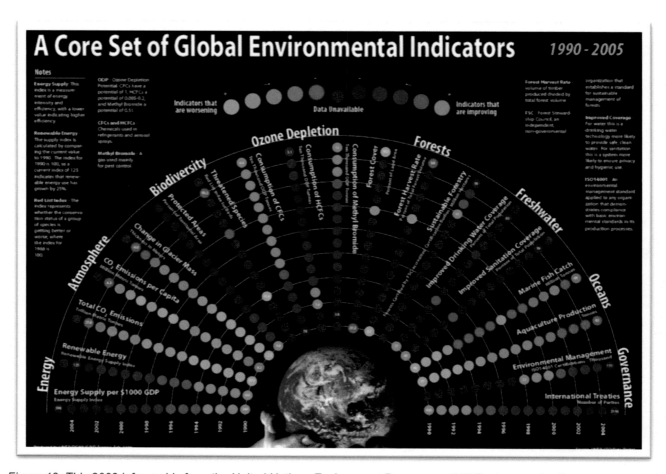

Figure 13: This 2009 infographic from the United Nations Environment Programme (UN Environment) offers an attractive scorecard for global indicators showing improvements and worsening of trends for major areas between 1990 and 1995.

Summaries, snapshots, reports

Data summaries and analyses can provide important information without requiring the in-depth planning for a longer report. A colorful one-page document, a trifold, or a folded 11x17 can provide the key points, whet the appetite for more details, and direct people to more comprehensive information online.

Brevity requires meticulous attention to details, a sharp focus on key points

We have put out indicators without thinking them through as much as we should have. The result is, we are trying to change the wrong levers. Thoughtfulness is essential in short-form reports where there is less space for context.

Kathy Pettit
National Neighborhood Indicators Partnership[72]

Strategies for success

Compiling indicators and publishing data is just the start. Indicators should also be useful and easy to apply and focus on users' needs.

You can come up with the best indicators, but if the community doesn't know about them or what to do with them, they're useless.

Karen Hruby
Truckee Meadow Tomorrow[73]

ADAPT REPORTING METHODS TO USER NEEDS

The structure of the project should be tailored to the users – and so should individual reports and publications. Reporting of indicators will be successful when projects consider the users' backgrounds, translate data to everyday language, counter user tendencies and bias, and design for peoples' natural limits.

Translate data to everyday language

Communicating research is like translating ideas to another language. As the translators of research concepts, the staff of indicators projects need to retain the meaning of the source "language" (data and indicators) while expressing ideas in accessible, everyday terms.

Consider these tips for translating to nontechnical language:[74]

Simpler is better: Concepts should be explained as simply as possible while keeping their meaning.

Focus on what users need to know: Avoid text that requires deciphering or hinders progress in absorbing meaning. Imagine that readers would need to explain what they learned to another person.

Reduce possible misinterpretations: Think of how words could be misinterpreted and adjust the writing to minimize that possibility. Write in concrete terms.

Counter user bias

Users bring prior knowledge, tendencies and bias to their understanding of indicators.

User tendencies include satisficing (getting "enough" for their purpose and moving on), holding expectations of experts, using contextual clues, resisting persuasion, and experiencing emotions connected to the data.[75]

Biases include confirmation bias, the tendency to see or understand only information that confirms one's personal belief, and anchoring bias, in which a user takes all following numbers in context to the first number they see.

Addressing bias and unhelpful tendencies are a part of ethical, precise, accurate reporting. Strategies to address user biases and tendencies include:

- Determine whether this is the right point in the conversation to introduce data
- Be complete and transparent in portraying data
- Do not start with conclusions against which someone could react strongly
- Identify and counter mistaken user beliefs
- Address uncertainty directly
- Explain key scientific or mathematical concepts
- Provide contextual information.

Design for user limits

People can only take in so much information at one time, let alone process it, understand it, and act on it. Indicators compete with all the other content users encounters each day. By the time somebody reads an indicators report, clicks a Facebook post, or scans a project's e-newsletter, they have likely already read multiple emails, seen dozens of advertisements, reviewed a few documents, and had many conversations requiring their full attention.

Table 5: To help cut through the noise here are responses to users' cognitive, objective, and subjective limits (adapted from the original source[76]).

You'd like users to...	Notice your indicators	Understand and remember the information	Feel invested and take action
But your users have...	Cognitive limits A.K.A. information overload (People are faced with more information than they can handle)	Objective limits (People can only take on a limited amount of information at once)	Subjective limits (People only take on new information when they are interested and motivated)
So, make sure to...	Share distinctive messages – not too many	Be clear, concise, simple, and consistent	Share information that is interesting, relevant, and personal

Consider these additional tips to work within audience limits. Notice how the tips use patterns – either following them or breaking them to make the message stand out. Patterns address cognitive load by requiring less mental energy.

- Data should be used sparingly to limit cognitive burden and presented in formats that are familiar to the audience (e.g., pie charts)
- The order or sequence of data will impact how information is remembered. For example, the first and last numbers presented are most likely to be remembered
- Identify and make numbers 'stand out' by showing how they are unique or novel Doing so will help demand attention and can promote newsworthiness.

Consider these questions:

- Are your data products adapted to user needs?
- What conventions or patterns can you draw on to address the limits of your users?
- Which of your messages could be made more clear, concise, and simple?
- How can you communicate about indicators in a way that is personal and relevant while remaining credible?

USE INCLUSIVE LANGUAGE

Indicators projects primarily convey information through words. Even when the vehicle of communication is visual, such as a map, words provide context and entry points to information. A project can use conscious, intentional word choices to increase understanding. Indicators are often used to build bridges and common understanding across diverse viewpoints. Therefore, an indicators project should choose words that are as accurate and inclusive as possible. Given the priority for indicators to be used in building strong communities, projects may opt for language that is positive and action-oriented – while still being precise and rigorous.

Conscious language is "the art of using words effectively in a specific context." The goal of conscious language is "not to be inoffensive or politically correct" but rather to "know your intention and evoke and provoke skillfully."[77]

For quality-of-life projects, meaningful provocation may include discomfort with the status quo and a call to action inspired by data. Unintended provocation through language is a distraction from broader goals. By understanding the impact and context of language through resources like the Conscious Style Guide, quoted above, indicators projects can make informed decisions about how to convey ideas effectively.

Inclusivity does not mean adding meaning to ideas or data. Rather, it means including a fuller range of the meaning that already exists in the data set or the context in which you share it. According to the Linguistic Society of America, "inclusive language acknowledges diversity, conveys respect to all people, is sensitive to differences, and promotes equal opportunities."[78]

Whether an indicators project produces its own data or uses data produced by somebody else, the project has an opportunity and responsibility to use words in an inclusive, intentional way. Everyone is included when we talk about inclusive language, but especially readers from groups that have historically been excluded by the conventions used and the assumptions made in a given field. It's about representing the people discussed in the report in ways that are fair and accurate and don't do harm—say, by justifying violence or reinforcing negative stereotypes."[79]

That opportunity is even greater when the original data source has not prioritized inclusivity.

TELL STORIES

> *For purposes of advocacy, a story is only as good as the impact it has on how audiences understand an issue or get involved... Advocates use a lot of numbers, expecting that those facts will lead to a breakthrough. It's by embedding the facts into a narrative that gives data a value.*
>
> Susan Nall Bales
> FrameWorks Institute[80]

Do you know how to report data in a way that inspires audiences to respond with passion?

Good data communication is about more than numbers and charts. As letters and words are building blocks for paragraphs and novels, individual data points are the building blocks for larger ideas and stories.

Research in the form of ideas, not pure data, is more likely to influence decision-making. Projects should produce actionable messages, not simply a set of indicators or a report.[81] Even a series of research reports can have a broader narrative context that builds up to a larger theme. If this is not within the capacity of the project, consider how to partner with other organizations or support users to connect with one another to take action.

Stories that stick

Stories are one of the principles behind "sticky ideas" (along with simplicity, unexpectedness, concreteness, credibility, and emotions). "Stories act as a kind of mental flight simulator, preparing us to respond more quickly and effectively."[82] Each data set holds a story. Every person involved in an indicators project, from the director to the data user, also comes to the work with stories in mind. Stories provide a structure to understand what is happening, why, and how we fit in. Including these stories breathes life in a report.

Consider:

- What story do you choose to tell about your research and your project's reason for being?
- What stories do your current data products tell?
- How can you use the power of stories to drive action, make ideas memorable, and support vibrant communities?
- Do your stories lead people to take action?

Framing

Every story has a frame: a structure that helps understand the world. Two simple frames are, "The world is full of problems that we have to solve," and, "There are solutions to problems if we know where to look." A deficit-based frame (the first) focuses on what is wrong, to the exclusion of what is going well. In contrast, an asset-based mindset (the second) includes the assets, strengths, and resources that can help address issues.

Providing a correct frame aids users in responding to data with an effective course of action. The wrong frame can lead to ineffective efforts – or even efforts that cause harm.

Words, images, and data points activate pre-existing frames in users' minds. For example, consider the different frames for a group described as "unemployed at rates far below the average" and a group that "holds untapped potential for our region."[83] Both phrases accurately describe data on employment rates, but one implies a regional deficit while the other evokes hope and points to a direction for investment.

The decision of how to compare groups also uses a frame. For example, a project may share data comparing two neighborhoods. If one neighborhood consistently stacks up poorly next to the other, a deficit framing can arise. That frame might lead people to see the "troubled" neighborhood as broken or failing – even when data exist that counter this narrative. To address this, consider framing comparisons in terms of excellence and gains within a particular group. For example, highlight positive trends within each neighborhood and describe its unique assets.

Words have power in the amount of airtime they receive. Rather than negating or describing a frame the project would like to move away from, simply replace it with the one the project seeks to advance.

The big picture

Projects that wish to inspire social change should direct users to take a broader view on social issues. Consider a report that includes one or more of the typical human interest stories in the telling of their community's story. The focus on one person or one moment may be memorable, but it captures only a small piece of the puzzle. While memorable, these stories highlighting individual experiences – both their challenges and triumphs – are a double-edged sword. From such stories, users could conclude that success and problems arise because of individual characteristics and not societal factors. The goal of an indicator project is often to shed light on the network of social factors involved in shaping a community. Thus, we recommended careful consideration of when and how anecdotes, profiles, and other similar methods of person-centered stories are used in reports.

As an alternative, projects should consider thematic stories. These stories describe shared values, context for social problems, and the capacity of people for addressing problems themselves.[84] The big-picture approach can provides information on the factors behind the problem, the impact on society, whether there is need to for change on a broader level (systems, policies, laws) and how to get involved.

MAINTAIN INTERACTION BETWEEN PROJECTS AND USERS

A new report or a dashboard update should be the occasion for more interaction with the community and its users. Supporting the written word with personal engagement is critical: a high level of interaction between indicators practitioners and users is likely to lead to greater data use. Attending community and municipal events provide opportunities to create greater awareness about the indicators and to make a case about the relevance and importance of the data.

It's really about getting the right information to the right person at the right time, and no report can do that alone.

Seema Iyer
BNIA[85]

We built relationships by being available. For example, a local radio DJ sent out an email looking for feedback. We have to work on their timeline and know what the journalists are looking for."

Ann Johnson
ACT Rochester[86]

Many projects emphasize the importance of live events and presentation as part of the reporting process. Some host their own events, while others mainly respond to requests for presentations. Many attend meetings and share the indicators during the course of conversation.

It is important to be intentional in pursuing and accepting opportunities. Projects may keep a record of the events they attend, splitting them out by topic area to understand which topics are resonating the most. This record can support planning for where to focus future efforts.

Conclusion

As community trends change, so do the ways in which users take in data. As in other areas, indicators projects do well to stay nimble. Plan ahead and remain open to finding new ways to report indicators.

With flexibility comes the continued need to prioritize credibility, accuracy and responsiveness to the wisdom, capacity and needs of the community. Quality reporting unites all of these elements to bring indicators to broader audiences and inspire action to support quality of life.

CHAPTER 8:
DATA TO ACTION

...there is no action without ownership. People own data that they've asked for, that they've produced, that they themselves analyze, that they themselves communicate

Terri Bailey
Remarks at the first Community Indicators Consortium conference[87]

Introduction

Community indicators projects are usually founded on a goal of collecting indicator data to spur changes that result in improvements to the community. As discussed in Chapter 2: Community Indicators Project Development, projects need not all aspire to be directly involved in moving the needle on some or all of the indicators (Fig.2 in Chapter 2). The will or the resources needed to actually move the needle on community conditions may not be available, or other organizations may already be in place to do that. However, all indicator sets should include actionable indicators.

This chapter offers suggestions on how to prepare a project for action, and, for organizations ready to go from data to action, an overview of how to proceed from the reporting of indicator data into a phase of mobilizing for action with an end goal of moving the needle. In addition to this information, Appendix B contains information about other useful reference materials.

Making lasting, community-level change requires changes at a high level (i.e., altering policy, systems, or the environment).[88] While it can seem daunting to think of effecting change at a structural level, the key is to find leverage points where change is both possible and impactful.[89] Identifying these leverage points depends on having good indicator data and a diverse, representative team of community members working together.

I think of this work as a race, a race for our communities, our nation, and more. But we in the community indicators field treat it more like a relay race. We see our job as running the first leg of the race in which we collect, produce and disseminate data and then we hand off to those who use the data to run the last leg of the race. We tell ourselves it is their job to use the data to promote equity and justice, to affect meaningful change in communities. We have convinced ourselves that our job is done once the hand off is complete. But the hand off is NOT the finish line. Anyone who has ever run a relay race will tell you that the first runner is as responsible for what happens at the finish line as the last runner.

Terri Bailey
at the first Community Indicators Consortium
conference in 2004[90]

Laying the groundwork

This report makes a few assumptions about steps projects have already planned for or taken to lay a foundation for action.[91] These core foundational pieces include:

Well-articulated, community-driven vision and goals for the project

The vision and goals set the direction of the project, reflect the community's priorities, and foster a sense of ownership by the community about the outcomes of the project. Community mobilization is most likely when there is a common and achievable goal related to improving conditions. Connecting the goals with action objectives from the start will facilitate taking action later. For more tools to support these stages of groundwork, see Community Engagement & Practical Tools for Community Engagement (Chapter 11 and 12).

A diverse network or coalition of local stakeholders who are passionate about the project and committed to using these findings to take action

As respected partners in the indicators process, these stakeholders (especially those who have been a part of the process) should be repeatedly engaged or kept updated so that they maintain interest. Additionally, having stakeholders who are representative of, and connected to, the community keeps the project fresh and relevant and enables the community to be ready to go from data to action. Also necessary for community change efforts is the capacity to cultivate collaboration, both by building trusting relationships and addressing any technical challenges. For more information in building these collaborations and coalitions, see Collaboration, Partnerships & Leadership.

Indicators that are leading, actionable, sensitive, and reflect the community's priorities

Indicators are the needle. They need to be responsive to the community and to actions taken to effect change. See Chapter 3: Criteria for Indicator Selection for a more in-depth discussion on what makes a good indicator.

Valid and reliable data

Data (plus an understanding of interconnected systems) help projects identify the right levers or entry points for action. For data analyses to produce valid and reliable findings, the indicators need to include sufficient information to be trusted and of value. For more, see Chapter 3: Criteria for Indicator Selection.

Widely-disseminated, compelling information

Detailed, accurate data are useless if no one sees them. In order to foster progress, data must be understandable and understood. From there, stakeholders' interest grows, as does their interest in having a stake in action. Reporting that connects indicator data to policy lays the groundwork for subsequent action steps that have an impact. For more information on presenting and disseminating indicator data, see Chapter 7: Reporting.

Data used by the community

Community capacity to access, share, and use data is often limited and must be continually built. The more community members who interact with the indicators, the more who will be motivated to engage in taking action.

Wicked Problems & the Need for Sensitive Indicators

Many of the issues identified by indicators (e.g., poverty, sustainability, equality, and health) are social or cultural problem that have stumped communities and institutions for decades and are still, in many cases, getting worse. They fall in the category of "wicked problems" [92] and are considered difficult to solve for as many as four reasons:

- incomplete or contradictory knowledge,
- the number of people and opinions involved,
- the large economic burden,
- the interconnected nature of these problems with other problems.

It is not to say that wicked problems cannot be solved or mitigated, but they will require 1) a deep understanding of cause and effect based on a thorough knowledge of the community, 2) the ability – and the resources -- to mobilize different sectors, and 3) a willingness – and the resources -- to stay involved, and keep a wide coalition involved, for a very long time.

Indicators that are sensitive and timely (see Chapter 3: Criteria for Indicator Selection) will help communities take smaller, more manageable bites of the problem and can show results in just a few years. This success is likely to improve the odds of keeping the coalition working to continue solving more community problems.

Focus on Future Users

Community indicators are a roadmap to guide action to improve community conditions. For this, a general audience is important to create awareness and build support and momentum for change and action. From the beginning, care should also be taken to make sure the indicators are seen, and ultimately used, by the users who will most directly effect change, e.g., provide funds for a program, change policies, or build something. Those users may be members of the community, or a variety of associated stakeholders such as funders, policy- or decision-makers, business leaders, etc. Even the best built indicators are not likely to be used, and therefore to effect change, unless care is being taken from start and throughout the indicator development process to:

- focus on the needs of potential users,
- report data in a way that is adapted to their needs, and
- promote meaningful interaction between researchers (or staff) and users over time.
- Intense, sustained interaction between researchers and users is associated with higher levels of use. Therefore, to make it more likely for people to use data:
- Begin with responsiveness: identify and get to know users expected to be involved in change-making; understand their needs and priorities; interact intensively with them; stay in touch. Select and design indicators projects that are focused on users' needs.
- Finish well: Consider which products and reporting formats will best meet users' needs (see Chapter 7: Reporting).

CNY Vitals: Knowing the Needs of Users

The CNY Vitals project recognizes that not everyone needs in-depth methodology information. Rather, some only need high-level facts and actionable takeaways.

At the same time, CNYCF works with users who appreciate specialized resources with a higher level of customization. Recognizing the different needs of these two user segments, CNY Vitals designed its website with a general audience section and a separate login-only section for "pro" users.[93]

From the design of an indicators project to the format of maps and graphs, every decision should take into account the needs of the end users. If the needs of those users conflicts with those of the community (e.g., a foundation needing more specific information than what is recommended for a general audience) consider two different products.

Interactive engagement is likely to be more effective than passive processes, regardless of the audience. Engagement goes beyond the indicator's brand and communications staff – it represents connections between individuals. This relationship-building happens through networking, friendship, and face-to-face interactions.

Interpersonal engagement is bolstered by organizational communications. Learn more about how to design a Communications plan in the Communications chapter (Chapter 10).

Moving to Action: Understanding what is at Stake

The first step in preparing to move from data to action is a game plan on the part of the community indicators project. Figure 13 outlines some important considerations.

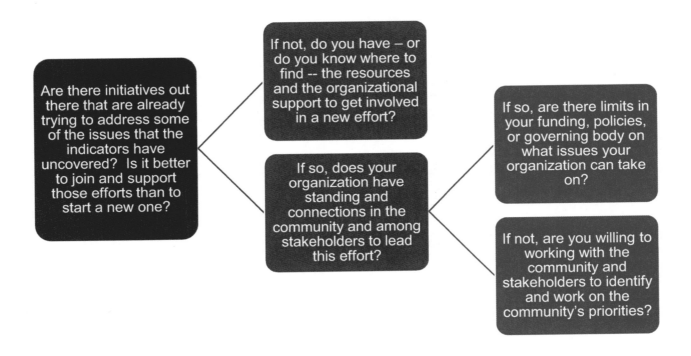

Figure 14: Understanding what is at stake – Game plan decision tree

Having considered the role, resources, and scope of involvement of your organization, you are now ready to mobilize for action.

Who to bring to the table?

A broad, inclusive group should have been engaged in the selection of indicators. A smaller group was likely involved in the collection and presentation of data on the indicators. In this stage, mobilizing for action, it will again be important to draw on collaborations and a community base. Among the many people involved, it is essential to have some who are "sparkplugs," [94] that is, people with the ability to energize and mobilize the community. Furthermore, projects will need participation from not only individual members of the community, but also individuals who are representing organizations.[95] The support of organizations and agencies – including representatives of the non-profit, government, and business sectors – can supply crucial resources and relationships with decision-makers that can facilitate action (for more, see the Partnership and Collaboration report – Chapter 9).[96] Given the challenging and complex nature of effecting change for most types of indicators, it is particularly useful to include certain key players. Depending on the focus of the indicator project, such key players may include: officials from local agencies, elected officials, healthcare and social service providers, education and childcare providers, community organizations, business leaders, faith communities, subject-matter experts, and, of course, community members with lived experience.[97] Practically speaking, it is also important to find those who are passionate, have a sense of urgency, and can commit to being engaged continuously for some time.

Collective Impact

One approach to action for communities is through a process known as **collective impact**. Through collective impact, community problems that are complex and may initially seem intractable (e.g., homelessness, a failing education system) are addressed in a multi-pronged, cohesive, visionary way by different agents within the community. A coalition to address one of the most urgent problems tracked by indicators may come together early in the indicator development process and hold together even as the needle is being moved different for other indicators.

The ideas of collective impact are also covered in Chapter 8, but, briefly, it is a group of key players in a community uniting around a set of shared goals (as measured by shared indicators), consistently communicating and coordinating their efforts to move the needle.[98] The collective impact model calls for a "backbone organization" – one dedicated, funded, independent organization that can serve to convene the others, provide support, and marshal resources, among other activities.[99]

There are three noted preconditions for a collective impact initiative: an influential champion, adequate financial resources, and a sense of urgency for change.[100] While collective impact initiatives have achieved some major successes, not all community indicators projects meet these preconditions, and a collective impact approach may not currently be feasible, but in communities that are able to undertake collective impact initiatives, it is a promising course of action.[101]

Organizing

Whether proceeding with a collective impact initiative or other approach, a steering committee or leadership council typically is needed to guide the movement. The steering committee is responsible for providing long-term strategic guidance, organizing specific working groups, monitoring progress, and being a public champion for the project.[102] It can be a continuation of the steering committee that oversees the community indicator development, or a new steering committee formed around a desire to move the needle on one or more indicators.

Figure 15 shows how participants may be structured in a collective impact model; similar structures without the backbone organization can also take place in communities. In addition to this broadly-focused steering body, individual taskforces or work groups are formed to address specific issues. These work groups are tasked with studying the data on an indicator, considering strategies, and potentially engaging in implementation activities. Some projects, such as JCCI, had two stages of work groups: one, termed a "study committee" was tasked with more thought work, whereas the second was tasked with implementation.

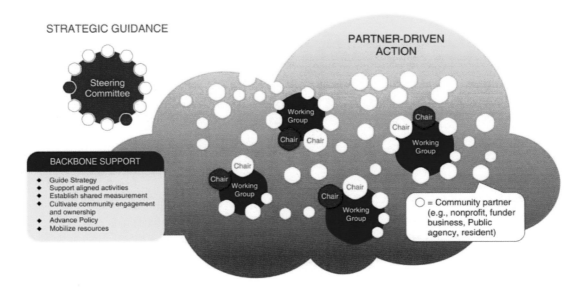

Figure 15. Typical structure of a collective impact initiative – Common Agenda and Shared Metrics, developed by FSG[103]

Practical advice for committees and work groups

Several logistical details will support a high-functioning work group:[104]

- Being led by at least two co-chairs who each represent a different stakeholder, but having these leadership responsibilities rotate throughout the group
- Meeting at least once a month, sometime more frequently in the early stages
- Comprising diverse participants
- Communicating and coordinating activities with other work groups
- Having strong internal communication
- Engaging with the steering committee, especially if issues arise

For more information about the forms and stages of collaboration, see the Collaboration, Partnership in Chapter 9.

A closer look: Organizing for action in Jacksonville

Jacksonville Community Council, Inc [JCCI], now the Citizen Engagement PACT of Jacksonville[105]

- Annually, 12-15 people on a program committee select issues they hope to actively address. Rather than trying to attempt the impossible and move the needle on everything at once, they select 1- 2 topics per year to address.
  - They winnow topics from numerous suggestions from the community through this process:
    - The program committee generates a short list (about 10 topics).
    - Then committee members prepare presentations on those topics to present to one another.
    - Then committee selects four to recommend to the JCCI board
    - Board makes final selection
- Once choices are made, topic-based volunteer committees meet weekly. These committees are expected to have tasks stretching over a year.
  - The first phase is information-gathering, drawing on knowledge of those in the committee, indicator project staff, local experts, and other stakeholders.
  - The goal is to arrive at a clear, evidence-informed definition of the problem that can inform potential solutions.
  - Then, committee considers possible solutions and their respective pros and cons. They prepare a briefing report of their recommendations that is publicly released, and ideally garners a lot of attention from the community.
- Then, each recommendation gets a new implementation task force, also populated by volunteers.
  - New time tables (often spanning multiple years)
  - Develop strategies to implement each recommendation

Transitioning from indicator data to an action plan

CLARIFYING THE PROBLEM

As noted in the JCCI example, a key part of the process is the statement of a problem or definition of a focal issue.[106],[107] Drawing upon the indicator data, community asset data, and community vision, the goal in identifying these issues is to specify leverage points where change is essential for achieving the desired community outcomes. It is important to note that a key quality of the identified issues is that it is possible to expect change given the resources that are available. There may be an issue that everyone feels is important, but if any systematic change that could address that issue is far beyond the capacity of the community, it is not productive to include that as a focal issue at this point. That is not to say that focal issues need to be *easy* to address; they may be challenging, but still possible and critically important to the well-being of the community.

In brainstorming issues, consider whether there were recurring themes across different indicator domains. Additional tips for facilitating the brainstorming process are available through the Community Toolbox.[108] From the brainstormed list, pare down to three to five cross-cutting issues. Remember that early success is important to building momentum and sustainability, and that success is more likely when efforts are concentrated on a handful of issues. Arrange these issues in an order that makes sense – this could be by order of urgency, or if action on some issues are contingent on progress in other areas, arrange accordingly. This list is now the basis of an **action plan**.

ENVISIONING A PATH TO CHANGE

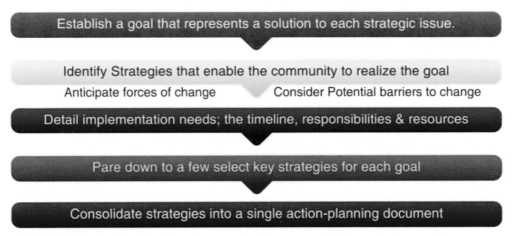

Figure 16: Steps in action planning

Once there is a prioritized list of issues, the next phase is to outline the specific steps that will help the community address those issues. For efficiency, this can be the responsibility of a work group alone; depending on the size of the group, it might even be useful to break into even smaller groups. The first step is to establish a goal that represents a solution to each strategic issue. Then, once there is a list of goals, identify strategies that enable the community to realize the goal. These strategies should anticipate the forces of change (i.e., factors that currently or potentially transform the community, such as demographic, economic, or policy changes[109]) and maximize the community assets that were previously identified. As strategies emerge, it is also important to anticipate and articulate potential barriers to change. Then, for each strategy, be specific in detailing the timeline, responsibilities, resources to be used, and other components of implementation. At this stage, if brainstorming has been robust, there are likely more detailed strategies than it is feasible to pursue. Some likely seem more achievable or important than others. The work group should select key strategies for each goal, and these strategies should be consolidated into a single action-planning document.

Characteristics of strong strategies

The Collective Impact Forum provides a planning tool[110] that outlines seven characteristics of strong strategies. They suggest that strategies:

- Be evidence-based (i.e., have research supporting the connection of the strategy to change in the outcome of interest)
- Build on and propel existing momentum
- Have a systems-level focus
- Have a possibility of effecting change on a large scale in the community
- Draw on collaborations (i.e., understand that many stakeholders are necessary but not sufficient)
- Be assignable to a champion
- Address disparities

In addition to these seven characteristics, they also recommend including a combination of strategies that can be completed in under a year (i.e., "quick wins") versus those that necessitate a longer time horizon.

Examples of approaches used in strategies

Strategies like these are used in communities across the country.

- New or expanded programming or services
- New partnerships or coalitions bringing together stakeholders
- New curriculum for schools
- New or restructured departments within the local government
- Changes to local codes/policies
- New ordinances
- New monitoring strategies
- New taxes levied for funding initiatives related to the focal issues
- New, permanent avenues of communication created (e.g., a 311 call center; reporting services)
- New pipelines for action (e.g., community members report roadway problems, and the reports are promptly integrated into a work order at the public works agency)
- Safety initiatives
- Property acquisitions[111] or new buildings (e.g., clinics, early child education centers)

Planning for implementation

Finally, with the planning work done, the foundation has been laid, and a project is ready to move into the **action cycle**. This work should continue with a small group who is tasked with overseeing the action cycle and keeping momentum going. Despite all the work that has been done identifying focal issues and specifying goals, there is one more step necessary in planning for action: developing specific objectives. Each level has gotten more specific, and objectives are now the precise tasks that need to be accomplished as stepping stones to achieving the project goals. One way of framing the specificity of these objectives is through the SMART (or SMART-C) framework, described below. These details will help you create an action plan to accomplish each objective, and in turn realize your goals. The action steps should address:[112]

- What actions will take place
- Who is responsible for the action
- A deadline for initiation, and specification of the duration of the action
- An indication of resources (i.e., money, personnel) needed

It is also important to take a step back and compare action plans for different objectives, making note of places where the work can be combined to maximize resources and efficiency. The creation of these action plans should draw upon the inventory of local resources and community assets conducted earlier; it may be that community organizations are already working toward or accomplishing some of the project objectives, and that realization of goals will happen much faster with cooperation, coordination, and support of existing community efforts. There are many planning tools that can help with this process. For example, County Health Rankings has an online Action Center[113] with activities and tools linked to each activity as well as partner guides for groups ranging from businesses to government. Detailed action planning guides on several topics (e.g., youth violence, child abuse, chronic disease) are available here.[114]

Ultimately, the plan for action should be seen as a plan for catalyzing change.[115] In other words, the goal is to promote a series of changes that connect to the overall vision (as opposed to delivering a specific program). This draws on the principle of Asset Based Community Development (ABCD), which notes that communities are already rich in abilities and prompts organizations to consider what community members can do entirely by themselves, where they may need support from organizations, and what actions are outside the scope of community resources.[116]

An ongoing cycle and a need for evaluation

Undertaking this process of moving from data to action is not meant to be a onetime event. These steps are really part of an ongoing cycle that continuously adapts to drive the community forward.[117] Recall the Community Indicators Development Process (Figure 17):

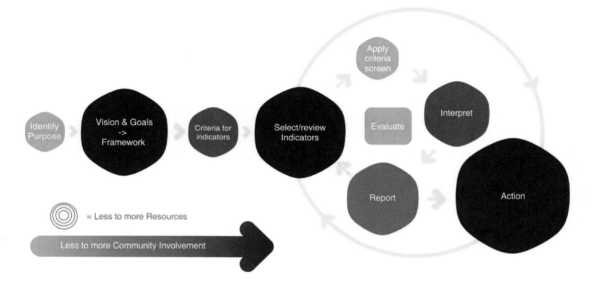

Figure 17: Community Indicators Development Process – The larger the shape the more resources needed; the darker the shape the more community involvement is necessary

Because the mobilization process is perceived as a cycle, learning from the past will prevent future mistakes. Thus, in an ideal scenario, the entire action planning and implementation process would be tracked and monitored. This information allows a group to identify progress and failures, but more importantly, learn whether a failure was a failure of the strategy or a failure to properly enact the strategy, which is crucial information for moving forward. Whether conducted internally (i.e., by someone within the group) or externally (i.e., by a third party), planning for evaluation should actually commence simultaneously with the mobilization process. Evaluations can assess both process (e.g., Were the necessary parties at the table? Were deadlines consistently met? What worked well?) and outcomes (e.g., Was change achieved?). Such knowledge is vital to informing ongoing and future efforts.

Supportive practices

In order to support community members throughout the action process, many communities have taken steps to build the capacity of local leaders. For example, community indicator projects have hosted events such as grant-writing training[119] and leadership development programs.[120] At a non-local level, projects may engage in a community of practice with other indicator projects to share best practices and lessons learned, troubleshoot challenges together, and see other communities in action through site visits.[121]

Another supportive practice arises when local philanthropies and non-profit funders, such as United Way, draw on indicators to decide how to allocate their funding.[122] Funders can explicitly ask prospective grantees to address which indicator or focal issue they will be addressing and how.

All [our] partners are required to connect their work to the SA2020 indicators, so when we connect individuals and partners to funders, they know they are also impacting community indicators. In fact, the City, the community foundation and several corporations only, or mostly, fund SA2020 partners.

Molly Cox
SA2020[118]

Challenges and possible solutions

Effecting change is rarely, if ever, easy. Below are some ways that indicator projects have worked around challenges in getting wide support for action.

➢ In some cases, it may be that the scope of the project is not ideal for taking action (i.e., key decision makers don't want to play when they would be held accountable for matters they have little control over) or that the geographies included in the community don't resonate with folks deeply enough to incite the necessary passion. For example, Sustainable Seattle initially saw little action on the regional indicators they had compiled. They shifted their focus to neighborhood-level indicators, and were able to get more people invested, which eventually paved the way for them to scale back up the regional level.[123] Figuring out where action is possible can be crucial to building momentum.

➢ While the ideals of collective impact are great, bringing that many key players to the table isn't possible in all communities. In Nevada, the TMT project enabled individual citizens to promote action through the "Adopt an Indicator" program, in which individuals agreed to be the community champion for an indicator. While this approach is unlikely to move the needle in the way that collective impact might, it excels at keeping community members engaged and feeling empowered to be part of the solution in their communities.[124] To identify prospective indicator adopters, consider the community asset map.

➢ Another approach used by TMT was compacts, or legal contracts, with partner organizations to outline their approaches to moving the needle on an indicator.[125] These partner organizations could contribute either by working toward direct changes that would affect the indicator or on upstream conditions.

➤ Community members may have different interpretation of indicator data, and thus different views on appropriate actions. Everyone is building an interpretation using their prior knowledge and expertise, which varies. One solution is to hold "data parties" or collaborative interpretation sessions where audiences work together to voice their interpretations and explanations for findings.[126]

➤ Other things to consider when presenting indicator data include audience habits and limitations, ranging from a tendency to lose interest if some insight or information doesn't come easily, to an expectation than an expert has "the right" answer or solution, to a general resistance to persuasion and need to stand their ground, to an assumption that correlation is synonymous with causation.[127] These tendencies can also be mitigated through a facilitated (i.e., someone guiding the conversation and helping to make the data accessible to those with less data literacy, among others) judgement-free dialog and conversation where community members' own expertise is emphasized.

PART II: THE NETWORK

CHAPTER 9:
PARTNERSHIP AND COLLABORATION

Introduction

Indicators reflect issues and opportunities in the lives and work of many varied and diverse community stakeholders. Indicators projects can play multiple roles in community improvement efforts: as a spotlight revealing issues for groups to address, a backbone to a broader coalition, and a frame of common language and understanding. Effective action arises when these diverse stakeholders come together. Collaboration helps organizations solve complex problems and adapt to changing environments.[128]

Consequently, collaboration and partnership, as well as leadership skills, have an important role to play at every stage of the community indicators development process. For example:

 To play a meaningful role in quality-of-life efforts, organizations managing indicators initiatives must collaborate with others.

*Craig Helmstetter
formerly with Minnesota
Compass[129]*

- Partnerships with a variety of organizations are needed to help identify the vision, goals, and priorities of an indicators project.
- A coalition of engaged stakeholders can provide important leadership in the community when it comes to taking action to move the needle on the indicators.
- Leadership brings together oversight, technical, or advisory committees made up of diverse stakeholders and organizations to support the indicator selection and interpretation stages. These groups need to be formed, nurtured, and sustained.

Partnerships may exist for a specific span of time or continue indefinitely. Partners may unite around a geographic area, issue, sector, or organization. Each partner provides resources to further a common cause.

Partnerships with external organizations may be especially beneficial for smaller indicators projects that are unlikely to have all the resources they need in-house. The main project staff of community-based organization may be expert in data analysis but may need local partners with strong relationships in the community to identify which issues to focus their analyses on. A foundation may provide financial capital and staff for a community indicators project but may still need to partner with an academic institution for research services. A community organization could outsource the analytic process while focusing their efforts on effecting community change. Corporate partnerships can open doors to funding and volunteer resources. The faith

community may have expertise and trust at the neighborhood level. The possibilities for partnerships are virtually limitless.

Additionally, many CI project practitioners noted that their engagement with other community organizations was an important part of their work. When CI project staff participate in different coalitions, it allows them to have their "ear to the ground" about what's happening across the community.

 Instead of pulling data, we want to contract that out and spend our time and efforts trying to move the needle.

Frank Ridzi
CNY Vitals[130]

Stages of Collaboration

Partnerships take many forms and vary in intensity. They cover a wide range of relationships between independent entities. The goal of partnership is to achieve greater value and impact than either entity could generate on its own. Partnership can also play a role in decision-making and support the creation of novel strategies to strengthen communities and address issues.

There are many ways for organizations to work together, ranging from less to more intense (Figure 17).[131] Scholars have described a continuum of collaborative practices; on the less collaborative end, partnerships may simply be two or more organizations communicating with one another about their activities. A next step might involve coordinating so that efforts aren't duplicated. In highly collaborative settings, organizations may offer well-integrated joint programming and work together to establish a new vision. Generally, as the extent of interaction increases, so do the needs for trust, interdependence, communication, accountability, organization, and commitment. These investments can translate into bigger rewards with regards to productivity (i.e., changes in policies, initiation of programs, and securing of resources) and project impact.

93

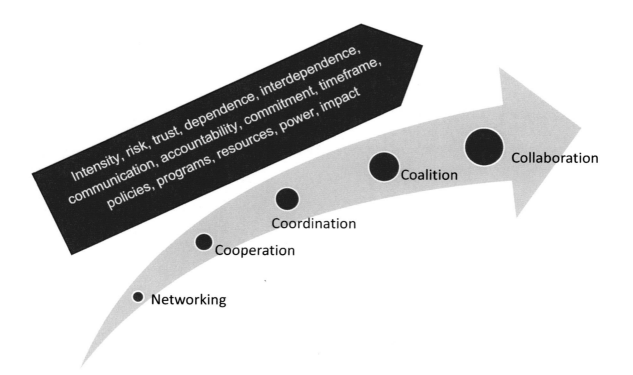

Intensity, risk, trust, dependence, interdependence, communication, accountability, commitment, timeframe, policies, programs, resources, power, impact

Networking

Cooperation

Coordination

Coalition

Collaboration

Figure 18: Stages of collaboration. Adapted from Hogue (1993).[132]

The types and strength of alliances needed by an indicator projects will vary depending on the stage of the project and current activities. Collaboration should further the goals of an indicators project – and of the other organizations taking part. However, each partnership requires an investment of time and resources. Thus, an indicators project should consider carefully and strategically the level of collaboration to invest in each partnership.

Case study: Spartanburg Community Indicators Project[133]

Spartanburg Community Indicators Project (SCIP) models multitiered collaboration between diverse sectors. SCIP plays a strong leadership role while equipping community organizations and partners to lead in specific areas.

PARTNERS IN LEADERSHIP

SCIP works with organizations from academic, philanthropic, nonprofit, and government areas. Two representatives from each of the seven sponsoring partners sit on the SCIP Cabinet which guides and sponsors the indicators project. Members include: The Spartanburg County Foundation, United Way of the Piedmont, Spartanburg County, University of South Carolina Upstate, Mary Black Foundation, Spartanburg Regional Foundation, and Spartanburg Area Chamber of Commerce.

STAKEHOLDER LEADERSHIP

In addition to the cabinet, community partners are engaged at several levels, including Indicator Area Leaders, Indicator Area Priority Groups, and Indicator Area Partners. As SCIP explains,[134]

> Indicator Area Leaders are the organizations or coalitions who have committed to organize community work around their specific Indicator Areas. This broad title includes everyone who is committed to work on outcomes in that Indicator Area. There are two sub-sets within this group: a guiding council for each Indicator Area Leader and representatives to the Indicator Area Leaders Council.
>
> 1. Indicator Area Leaders, depending on their structure, are guided by councils or boards who meet regularly to check on progress, set goals, identify anyone who may need to be included in the work but isn't yet, and provide feedback on and for the Project through the SCIP Director. The Council is a small group that guides the work of the Indicator Area Leader through its Priority Groups who in turn guide the work of Indicator Area Partners.
> 2. Two representatives from each Indicator Area Leader's guiding council serve on the Indicator Area Leaders Council. The purpose of this Council is to facilitate communication among the seven different Indicator Area Leaders since all of the work is intertwined. Finding areas where working together impacts two or more Indicator Areas and ultimately the community is a priority of the Project's efforts to assist in more effective and efficient use of the community's resources.
>
> Indicator Area Priority Groups focus on specific issues within the broader Indicator Area, e.g. Water Quality & Supply within the Natural Environment Indicator Area. These groups are the vehicle for setting goals, identifying impactful work and sharing information in the community. They are also the entry point for new Indicator Area Partners to get involved and align their ordinary work and activities with the broader goals determined by the Indicator Area Priority Groups and the Indicator Area Leaders guided by Indicator Area data.
>
> Indicator Area Partners are any public or private organizations, businesses, or citizens who are committed to working with the Indicator Area Priority Groups and using the SCIP data to improve outcomes in a specific area for Spartanburg County.

WHAT TO EXPECT: LIFESPAN OF COLLABORATION

The most visible parts of collaboration are the results it produces, but those results generally follow several stages of collaborative group development[136] (Figure 18). To give you a sense of what to expect, in this section, we outline one possible lifecycle for a collaboration.

While the stages are presented here as a linear progression, we might consider them as part of a cycle. Collaborative efforts rise, fall, and intersect with other initiatives. They may return to earlier stages or stagnate at one stage. Every stage comes with different activities and questions. But from assembling the members to creating shared norms and processes, these stages lay the foundation for greater joint impact.

We see all our users and stakeholders as partners in crafting something that's usable. If we operate in a vacuum as researchers, giving what information we think is best, then we're going to fail in terms of sustainability, relevance and being useful.

Allison Liuzzi
Minnesota Compass[135]

Figure 19: Stages of collaboration development. Adapted from Rocha, H., & Miles, R. (2009). A Model of Collaborative Entrepreneurship for a More Humanistic Management. Journal of Business Ethics

Form & storm

In the initial stages, participants ask whether collaboration will be useful to meet a particular outcome (e.g., fully engaging a community in measuring progress; moving the needle on an indicator). They consider vision, mission, and strategic alignment in relation to the expected outcomes of the collaboration. Members and potential members

consider whether joining is in their best interest. The members **form** into a group, building momentum and energy as they begin to articulate common goals.

During this stage, questions about logistics can dominate (e.g., who will pay for meeting space?). In the forming stage, consider how to build energy for the collaborative's vision. A kick-off event, press release, or ribbon-cutting can publicize the work and compel new members to join.

The **storming** stage, characterized by some level of conflict, can happen when the group's ambitions meet the realities of operational and cultural constraints. Storming is a natural part of many group efforts. For example, a conversation about budgeting priorities may reveal that collaborative partners have different values and approaches. Later changes to the status quo—staffing, resources, community events—can lead a group to re-enter the storming phase.

For us, collaboration is about evolving and creating a space for innovation – allowing organizational partners, who aren't traditionally able to come to the table together, to look at areas they want to impact in an innovative and cross-cutting way.

Sam Joo,
Magnolia Community Initiative[137]

Disagreement can lead to valuable conversation, but too much conflict may cause an effort to stall out. Understanding that this is a normal step in the process and carefully considering how to address potential conflicts and keep the group focused on shared goals will help groups survive this stage.

Norm

Decision-making and impact come more readily when a relationship is built on a strong foundation.[138] A lack of mutual understanding and trust can harm the chances of success. Norms (i.e., a system of shared values, processes, and understanding) support strong relationships and impact over time. In the **norm** phase, members determine their roles, decide on goals, and set standards to carry out the work of the collaboration. Establishing norms and values may happen consciously or may naturally take place as the partners begins to work together.

Norms include power dynamics, such as who has informal and formal authority to make decisions; who needs to be present for decisions; and what level of influence members have on the direction of the collaboration. Norms relate to communication styles and format but also to cultural aspects relating to tone of conversation, how to manage conflict, and instinctive expressions such as dress and where meetings are held.

As a collaboration determines its norms, it will create **order** for its work. Ordering includes formal, shared processes: How will members communicate? Does the group have a physical headquarters? Where are digital files stored? What is the collaboration's legal status? How will it pay for its activities? How often will members meet? Does the collaboration require a public presence, with accompanying infrastructure (e.g., website, social media, press releases)? Will it have its own staff?

The key thing is to make sure roles and responsibilities are clear, and black and white; and everybody is accountable for what they're doing.

Jennifer Temmer
Peg[139]

Understanding, articulating, and intentionally setting the norms within a collaboration becomes even more critical as the diversity of membership increases. Each person and organization bring their own pre-existing norms to the table. Without a shared understanding of how the work will proceed, members may feel confused, unproductive, or left out.

The practices of self-organizing, mobilizing, and drawing on shared resources and processes are all important parts of building up a collaborative environment.

Perform

The next stage of a collaborative is the **perform** stage: taking action to reach the outcome that was intended when the partners set out to build a collaboration. If the **form** stage represents the question "Who?" and the **norm** stage answers the question "How?" the **perform** stage explores "What?"

This is the desired stage for organization. The foundation of trust and of shared understanding of the issue can now be harnessed to create innovative responses and ideas. The results of such collaboration may be beyond the members' initial investment, helping to create something that could not have been achieved by any one of the member organizations working alone. Here, the group marks positive change in the issue or community in which it came together to perform. Performance can be punctuated by celebration, reflection, and adjustment.

Adjourn

Every collaboration has a different trajectory. For example, collaborations around these goals would have different outcomes:

- Address a temporary need or opportunity
- Build capacity to support an ongoing need
- Create connections for ongoing collaboration among groups in the same area

In one case, the collaboration can mark its end date very clearly – the collaborative has completed its work once it has addressed a need. However, for ongoing needs, the collaboration may continue to operate. Over time, the collaboration may encounter challenges and opportunities requiring an intentional space to focus and re-invest.

Applying the cycle

Collaboration rarely follow this cycle exactly. An effort may stall out from lack of funding, leadership, or vision. Or it may return to an earlier point in the cycle because of new leadership or changes in the issue area that prompted it to form. New members may be screened and added throughout the process. Elements from the stages might take place at the same time or in a different order. An alliance may work toward a goal, adjourn the work, and form a refreshed group to work on another goal. Some efforts will raise awareness and build membership, leading to microstages of norming as they continue to produce results.

Throughout this process, give thoughtful consideration to a partnership's transition. Take time to learn from the work, share knowledge, celebrate success or process failure, tie up or pass along loose ends, and plan next steps.

Case study: ACT Rochester[140]

This project adapted to changing conditions while providing indicators to build up the state of New York.

GROUNDED IN COLLABORATION

FORM and STORM: ACT Rochester began as a joint venture of Rochester Area Community Foundation and the United Way of Greater Rochester. Five years into the project, United Way decided to focus their funding on direct services, so the partnership dissolved. Despite the major change in funding, ACT Rochester has leveraged other resources to continue their work. The Center for Governmental Research is also a key partner by contributing the research and analysis.

NORM: The partners considered what they wanted to do and who their key audience would be. They decided they would strive to change the culture of how problems were solved in the community. This conversation led to ACT Rochester's tagline: *Learn. Connect. Act.* The primary organizational partners navigated the challenges of working across different organizational cultures.

PERFORM: Together, the organizations developed the structure, funding, and data infrastructure of the project.

SHIFTING ROLES

The roles of the collaborative members shifted over time – a natural evolution as resources, goals, and the environment changed. ACT Rochester is now a program of the Rochester Area Community Foundation. The project continues to have an impact along the lines of the vision cast by the original group.

Collective impact

Collective impact is a framework for collaboration designed to address issues that are deeply rooted and might otherwise seem insurmountable. Rather than just focusing on one or two strategic partnerships, collective impact initiatives focus on moving the needle by bringing together many key stakeholders across a community. In this setting, processes and results "are emergent rather than predetermined, the necessary resources and innovations often already exist but have not yet been recognized, learning is continuous, and adoption happens simultaneously among many different organizations."[141] The core ideas of collective impact are that participating organizations will unite around a **common agenda,** commit to frequent and **open communication**, agree on **shared measurement** approaches, and align their efforts in "**mutually reinforcing activities**." All collective impact efforts should also identify a "**backbone organization**" that has the skills and capacity to coordinate the initiative.[142,143] Much has been written and studied about collective impact that goes beyond the scope of this work. Visit the reading packet put together by Truckee Meadows Healthy Communities,[144] or Collaboration for Impact.[145]

Collective impact takes place across several phases. Each phase includes components for success, detailed in Table 6.

100

COMPONENTS FOR SUCCESS	PHASE I GENERATE IDEAS & DIALOGUE	PHASE II INITIATIVE ACTION	PHASE III ORGANIZE FOR IMPACT	PHASE IV SUSTAIN ACTION & IMPACT
Governance & infrastructure	Convene community stakeholders	Identify champions and form cross-sector group	Create infrastructure (backbone and processes)	Facilitate and refine
Strategic planning	Hold dialogue about issue, community context, and available resources	Map the landscape and use data to make case	Create common agenda (common goals and strategy)	Support implementation (alignment to goals and strategies)
Community involvement	Facilitate community outreach specific to goal	Facilitate community outreach	Engage community and build public will	Continue engagement and conduct advocacy
Evaluation & improvement	Determine if there is consensus/urgency to moving forward	Analyze baseline data to identify key issues and gaps	Establish shared metrics (indicators, measurement, and approach)	Collect, track, and report progress (process to learn and improve)

Table 6: The four phases of collective impact (Collaboration for Impact, accessed 2017) [146]

The most critical factor for collective impact is an "influential champion."[147] This champion, or group of champions, must also be a key player in the community. The person or people in this position must have enough clout to not only bring together other top-level community leaders, but also keep them engaged over time.

The benefit of indicators to collective impact goes beyond indicators as shared measurement. Indicators projects can inspire the formation of a collective impact initiative. A project may be created for or invited into a collective impact effort that is already operating. Indicators projects can support collective impact in many ways: committee meetings, reporting of data, strategic planning support, and participation in community events, to name a few.

Case Study: Central New York Community Foundation (CNYCF)

PARTNERSHIP IN ACTION: COORDINATED DATA SYSTEMS AND A BROADLY-FOCUSED CLIENT NEEDS ASSESSMENT

Data is a fundamental part of community indicators projects. The better the data, the more informative and useful the indicators are. A commitment to coordinated data systems is a triumph of successful partnerships.

In an extension of their commitment to tracking movable indicators, CNYCF, as part of their collective impact process, has initiated a coordinated data system across local agencies. They introduced a needs assessment survey that diverse agencies administer to their clients. The agency enters and geocodes the data (which does not include personal identifiers) to a census tract, which gets shared into a central database. This allows other partners to see where clients have certain needs. For example, a program focused on adult education might collect a high volume of needs assessment surveys from clients who indicate unmet mental health needs. The use of the broad needs assessment survey and the sharing of that data would allow a partner agency who does offer mental health services to identify areas of the community where they could offer valuable supports.

The advice from Frank Ridzi, Vice President Community Investment of Central New York Community Foundation, was to start small in these data-sharing efforts. Figure out how to make it work with your local partners, and then begin to scale it up.

CREATIVE WAYS TO ENGAGE PARTNERS

Another promising initiative happening at CNYCF is their "data Friday." It evolved from a performance measures management community where nonprofits who wanted to be better at managing and using their data met monthly for technical assistance. Some instruction in open-source programming (R) was offered, which was of interest to people. From there, it has grown into a group of folks who focus both on the technical aspects of data wrangling for local governmental and non-governmental organizations and the more strategic aspects of what the different agencies are doing. People attending the meetings discuss the data they have, the way they collect it, and work together to figure out how to make it accessible and meaningful to other organizations trying to move the needle on indicators. Dr. Ridzi says that this is a "trust group" where different community organizations are building camaraderie and solid professional relationships with one another.

KEY PARTS OF THE PROCESS

For CNYCF, key parts of the process of building an effective collective impact effort to make meaningful change for Central New York residents involved:

1. Getting funding

2. Identifying a backbone organization

3. Identifying issues and being strategic about an area to start with on efforts to move the needle in the community.

4. From there, pulling in the organizations that have been working in that area – service providers, local government agencies, community development groups, etc., but building in a way that is purposeful while also cautious and strategic. The backbone organization must make it clear that the collaboration has focus and is headed for action. "It's like building a campfire; you don't want to throw heavy wood on right away and smother it. Build cautiously and strategically until you have a roaring flame."[148] This "flame" is an early win of the collaboration.

5. Publicize the win.

6. Continue to build the collaboration with others who can help move the needle.

Success factors

Forming productive collaborations can be challenging. While nothing guarantees a positive outcome, research has shown there are factors likely to be present when collaboration is working.[149] Four key elements of successful collaborations relevant to indicators projects include:[150]

1. Mutual understanding and trust

Trust is key to the success of collaboration and may be the most important factor in successful collaboration; without it, alliances may not fulfill the promise of their full potential.[152]

While the intent to build strong relationships must also translate into impact, progress moves at 'the speed of trust.'

Frank Ridzi
CNY Vitals[151]

This underscores the importance of investing in the initial stages of collaboration, where clear norms and communications standards are established, and in developing good leadership skills, since leadership through trust-building occurs even before collaborative members form and assemble. These trust-based relationships are then built and sustained throughout the life of the collaboration.

2. Members see the collaboration as in their self-interest

Self-interest is a natural part of collaboration. After all, collaboration requires resources; without a corresponding benefit, participation would not be worth the investment or risk. If the partnership seems to be lagging, consider whether it truly serves not just your goals, but also the goals of the key members.

Perception is important. Consider how to not only provide benefits but convey them to members in a meaningful way. These activities reinforce the value of the collaboration.

Cultivate relationships with staff, make friends with people who do not realize how important their work is. They're lower on the org chart, but those are the folks who allow us to do our job. Help them; value the jobs they do.

Seema Iyer, BNIA[153]

3. Multiple layers of participation

Every link between organizations strengthens their bond. Consider how to engage various staff of partner organizations. Think carefully about how and when to communicate to each group, and what each will find valuable.

For example, executive leadership may not be interested in the nuts and bolts of indicators, preferring high-level syntheses to inform decision-making, or invitation to decision-making meetings rather than brainstorming sessions. However, people working directly with data may value participation in technical meetings or sharing of information about related data efforts.

4. Open and frequent communication

Being a volunteer network, often we have to compete with other priorities of partner organizations. Since we don't directly provide funding for our partners, we have to offer something that's of value to each organization. We highlight partners, communicate success stories, and track partner engagement over time.

Sam Joo
Magnolia Community Initiative[154]

"Out of sight, out of mind" should not become the model for collaboration. Instead, plan regular, targeted communications. Collaboration leaders may send official updates to membership, while members may communicate with one another informally. Take note of the needs of each member, and the frequency with which they would appreciate updates on the work.

Appendix C offers a further summary of factors that influence the success of a partnership. For more information on engaging community members and organizations, see the Community Engagement section (Chapter 11).

Potential partners

Each project will draw from a different set of potential partners, depending on the project's focus, location, and maturity. For example, a project working on health equity may collaborate with public officials, healthcare providers, activists, and patients. When the project begins a strategic planning process, it may draw on the wisdom of facilitators, organizational leaders, and the people who use the indicators.

Try creating a list of the people and groups that are an intuitive fit for collaboration with a project. It is best to think broadly and remember to include people who are the beneficiaries of a system even if they typically have little power (students or patients, for example). When building lists of potential partners, inquire with colleagues, partners, and even outsiders to see how they assess the collaborative partnerships. They may have ideas for making new connections.

Collaborative leadership

The ability to inspire others and manage processes is critical to collaboration and partnership. Relationship-building, sustainability, and impact rely on strong, adaptive leadership from indicators projects and their staffs.

Leaders come in many forms. Given the wide-ranging work of indicators projects, collaborative leadership is often desirable. Collaborative leaders are those who have accepted responsibility for building – or helping to ensure the success of – a diverse team to accomplish a shared purpose.[155] Rather than creating a rigid hierarchical organization, they build capacity and foster a culture of distributed leadership that dramatically increases the collaboration's efficiency, effectiveness, and sustainability. Such leaders balance the "power to get things done with the love to make all boats rise."[156]

Collaborative leaders display these qualities:[158]

- Willingness to take risks
- Eager listening
- Passion for the cause
- Optimism about the future
- Ability to share knowledge, power, and credit

Gradually, effective leaders work with partners to help them identify and give voice to "their deeper aspirations."[159] Additionally, leaders who are championing large, cross-cutting projects must be able to:

- See the larger system,
- Foster reflection and more generative conversations, and
- Shift the collective focus from reactive problem solving to co-creating the future.[160]

> " We have tried to target community-based banking when we release the Vital Signs. Not only could they support the project monetarily, but they have – or could have – some of the biggest impact with respect to community development. So we host a pre-release breakfast with a growing list of community bankers.
>
> *Seema Iyer, BNIA[157]*

The leader should ensure that members of the collaborative acknowledge and build upon successes that they have had together. These successes should be a platform on which the

confidence to go forward together is built. As they envision the future together, the leader should guide them towards a model of being less reactive and more proactive. However, the transition from reactivity to proactivity is more than just building inspiring visions. Leaders must also help everyone face potentially difficult truths about the current reality, then leverage that discord between the ideal and reality to fuel the creation of truly new approaches.[161]

Case study: Peg[162]

Based in Winnipeg, Canada, the Peg community indicator system provides high-level leadership while working with community members from across various sectors. Leadership, decision-making, and resources are shared among the partners.

COLLABORATION & SUPPORT

Peg is a partnership between the International Institute for Sustainable Development (IISD) and United Way Winnipeg. Each organization brings its own priorities and ways of working to the table. "We have the same value and vision for what we want Peg to be, but we have different ways of getting there," says Jennifer Temmer, Project Officer at IISD and Team Lead for Peg.

A priority for Peg is to seek financial support from across all sectors, including government (municipal and provincial), business, health, and non-profit organizations.

SHARED LEADERSHIP

Peg's Advisory Group is comprised of senior leaders from a variety of sectors and provides overall guidance and oversight. Peg communicates at least quarterly with the collaborative members, and provides a yearly assessment on indicators. The reports help everybody understand the collaborative's current work and provide written documentation to use in evaluation.

When it comes to participating in other initiatives, Peg chooses its representatives carefully. "It depends on the group and what they need," says Temmer. United Way takes the lead on an initiative to end homelessness because of its social connections and experience dealing with social issues, while IISD leads the way on work related to the environment or planning and the Sustainable Development Goals.

"Of late, we've been doing a lot of work with the local chamber of commerce," Temmer says. "The CEO of the United Way and our director here at the IISD have been engaging on that profile of our portfolio. It requires a different level of leadership."

COMMUNITY PARTNERSHIPS

For Peg, the project's users can also be collaborators. While Peg has a broad audience, the most well-defined audience is the school system. They work with the Ministry of Education and their sustainable development curriculum for high school students. There are two social studies courses used across the Winnipeg Educational system as well as across the province that focus on Peg data. Students use the data to better understand the communities where they live and then develop action projects based on what they've learned.

Indicators projects are well-suited to creating the space for collective intelligence to emerge. Stakeholders who do not appear to have much in common can unite around indicators, setting the stage for conversation and shared learning. Conversations about measuring quality of life often begin to move toward solutions and collaborative vision-casting.

With time, commitment, and a willingness to learn through failure, a person can develop the core leadership abilities needed to bring people together to work collectively toward a vision for the future. Developing the ability to lead is supported by engaging people across boundaries, building a personal toolkit, and connecting with peers. For indicators projects, learning may take place with others in the indicators field, or people who share the same geographic or topic interest. Developing leaders can find support and connect with other leaders by consulting the indicators project database at the Community Indicators Consortium website (http://communityindicators.net/indicator-projects).

Magnolia Place Community Initiative: Building Leadership Capacity in the Community

Staff, particularly those at the manager level, at MCI partner organizations have the opportunity to participate in a MCI Fellowship Program that supports personal and professional development. The Fellowship meets monthly over several months, and as of 2018, MCI had trained five cohorts.

Topics covered ranged from theories of change to measurement systems and tracking changes that lead to impact. Fellows also participate in a group project, thereby strengthening not only their skills but also their professional network. By the end of the program, the Fellows have advanced their leadership skills, built new relationships, and are poised to become "tremendous advocates" for the community.[163]

CHAPTER 10: COMMUNICATIONS

Introduction

Communication plays a role in every part of a project's life, helping engage and motivate the community, develop and sustain partnerships, share information, and spur action. Communications are involved at every scale, from conversations between individuals to websites that reach thousands of people.

This chapter provides information related to communications' planning, channels, and measurement.

Communications planning

Every indicators project or data initiative should begin with the end user in mind.[165] Communications planning should happen at the same time as the planning of the project itself. Consider who cares about the project, what do they want to know about it, and what form of communication will help them get more involved.

Communications forms half or more of what we do on Compass. Communications means being part of communities that we hope use this resource, and engaging in all sorts of forms of outreach to make sure people know who we are--our identity, what we do and don't provide--and coming up with strategic communications plans to target specific outcomes.

Allison Liuzzi
Minnesota Compass [164]

Communications plans should be efficient and straightforward. A good plan saves time in execution and helps a team's efforts build toward a unified goal. A plan will provide structure as you respond to the questions of "What?" "To whom?" "By whom?" "How?" and "With what effect?"[166]

Include the right ingredients

Plan formats vary, but all include key ingredients: objectives and strategies, audiences and messages. The elements below can be adapted for a variety of settings and projects.

> *The first thing you've got to do is decide what you want the indicators project to do and who your key audience is.*
>
> *Ann Johnson*
> *ACT Rochester[167]*

Objectives: What do you hope to achieve or change with each communications element? Communications objectives should be clearly defined, achievable, and measurable. For example, success could mean that local policy makers and funders know about, and use, the indicators project, or a consensus by the community about what priorities to address. What small- and large-scale goals will your work drive toward? Those objectives should align under the larger goals of the project.

Strategies: How will those objectives be achieved? Each objective may include several strategies. The following elements are all part of the development of the strategies.

- **Target audiences:** With whom do you want to communicate? Audiences are made up of different groups of stakeholders, each with their own needs and preferences. When deciding who the audience is, ask the following questions: 1) Who can act on the basis of the information we are about to share? 2) Who can influence those who can act? And 3) With which of these target audience(s) can we expect to have the most success and what message can most directly reach them?[168]
- **Key messages:** What are the key messages you would like your audience to take away? Decide on no more than three. These are more than a marketing line; a message is a simple and clear idea that acts as a guiding principle for all kinds of communications[169].
- **Channels and tactics:** Through what means will you communicate (e.g., email blasts, Twitter, workshop)? Consider how channels can work together to reach users in a variety of ways.
- **Media:** Some projects lend themselves well to media coverage. Do your audiences include journalists? If not, make a list of media you would like to reach. Do your audiences *consume* media? If so, make a list of the media sources most likely to influence them, including social media.

Timeline and roles: The plan should have a principal owner—somebody with the main responsibility for implementing it, sharing changes, and making updates as timelines and requirements shift. An overall schedule for the communications plan implementation and names of responsible parties for each step helps with the overall success of the plan.

Resources, constraints & opportunities: Overall organizational budget, staff or volunteers' time need and availability, existing skills and human resources, and restrictions or commitments with partners and other influencers (e.g., a sponsorship agreement) need to be considered as part of the plan.

Craft strong messages

Remember to create strong messages that sticks in peoples' minds. "Leaders will spend weeks or months coming up with the right idea but then spend only a few hours thinking about how to convey that message to everybody else," says Chip Heath, author of *Made to Stick*. "It's worth spending time making sure that the lightbulb that has gone on inside your head also goes on inside the heads of your [audience]."[170]

Think about messages as solutions to problems. Table 7 describes the characteristics of good messages in this way.

Problem	Solution: Make your messages...	Goal: Ensure that people...
Information overload People are frequently faced with more information than we can handle	Distinctive Few in number	Notice
Objective limits People can only take on a limited amount of information at once	Clear Concise Simple Consistent	Understand Remember
Subjective limits People only take on new information when they are interested and motivated	Interesting Relevant Personal	Care Act

Table 7: Characteristics of a good message. Source: Pinnacle Public Relations Ltd 2009

Build the Framework

A communications plan will be more effective with a strong infrastructure behind it.

Consider these supporting elements:

User stories: Each project will have their own target audience. In planning for communications, one helpful approach is to work through the need of key members of that target audience. Imagine (or ask, when possible) the needs of each type of key stakeholder. Then develop a short, simple description of communication needs told from the perspective of that person – this is the "user story." This may include the user's goals, obstacles, and how that type of person prefers to engage with the project. Projects can refer to the (hypothetical) user stories to help team members relate to users and keep communications planning relevant, grounded, and useful.

For example, one user story may represent funders. The funders' goal when interacting with the indicators project is to find out information to use in grantmaking. They have limited time to research issues, and they prefer to get high-level information through face-to-face meetings. They likely appreciate relationships with people who hold formal leadership positions and seek ways to strengthen the foundation's presence in the community.

A project designing for this user may spend less time on an intricate online data tool, and more time maintaining a CRM (Customer Relationship Management) tool to ensure they do not miss opportunities to be in touch.

Style guide: A style guide is a reference document providing guidelines for all style-related decisions, from formatting to language use. From colors and fonts, to the way you describe your work, these will save time and add professional polish to everything you produce. Particularly when many people are involved and multiple documents are made over time, a style guide will save everyone time and energy. Furthermore, it helps ensure that a project presents a consistent, recognizable identity. A basic style guide can be easily created in-house and added to as needed, or a hired consultant can create (and possibly implement) a more involved one.

Calendar: A calendar organizes the content you plan to share, along with the timing and form. For example, the first Tuesday of every month might have a short "coffee break" webinar highlighting one indicator, with a follow up email that goes out that Wednesday to the list of e-newsletter subscribers.

> *We generally put out media releases monthly or every two months to drive info and get articles in the newspaper about different indicator topics. We put out a regular, annual report to dive deeper on a number of indicators."*
>
> *Jennifer Temmer*
> *Peg[171]*

Customer Relationship Management Software (CRMS): Customer Relationship Management Software keeps contacts organized and allows tracking of how they have interacted with your communications. There are free resources like Excel, low-cost options like Highrise or Airtable, or a more robust systems like RaisersEdge. Salesforce, a very powerful CRMS, offers free accounts to nonprofits and integrates with tools like MailChimp and Constant Contact.

Communication channels

Methods of communication will depend on the goals and resources of each project. Different projects and different situations require an array of tools. Communications experts talk about different forms of communications tools and channels, including owned, earned, and paid media, as well as events and publications (Table 8). Owned media refers to content that a project controls, which is unique to its brand. Earned media refers to media exposure through word of mouth, like when someone from the project is interviewed on a radio show or for an article. Paid media refers to anything a project pays for to increase exposure and boosts the efforts of owned and earned media. The array of tools for linking up with audiences is almost limitless, particularly as new technologies are developed.

Some methods communicate information in one direction: from the project to its audience. Others are bidirectional, looping, or networked: the communication flows between project and audience, partners, and other stakeholders. Events (Table 8) can be particularly helpful in getting back-and-forth communication.

Events	Owned media	Earned media	Paid media	Publications
Participation in others' events	Public service announcements	Data used by media	Public displays (e.g., billboards)	Interactive maps and visuals
Conferences	Newsletters and e-newsletters	Editorials	Paid promotions	Books & book chapters
Meetings	Blogs	Interviews	Advertisements	Brochures, flyers and pamphlets
Open houses	Microsites	Media coverage		Fact sheets
Live-streaming	Press releases			Infographics
Presentations	Social media			Articles
Table displays	Websites			Posters
Webinars	Brand identity			Reports
				Zines

Table 8: Sample communications tools and channels on which indicators projects have drawn.

Indicators projects interact with the communities in which they operate, influencing other organizations and being influenced in turn. Both indicators projects and communities are influenced by broader trends as well. In this view, indicators are one part of an interconnected system of thought.[172] When indicators projects adapt their work to the decision-makers who use the data, the decision-makers become more attuned to data and analysis.[173]

Each tool or channel comes with a different set of options for cost, thoroughness, size, quality, etc. Knowing the benefits and limitations of each approach and when to use them depends on the project, its goals, its audience, and the kinds of data that are available.[174] Effective use of communications channels will include strategic decision-making based on messages, resources, and other elements of a communications plan.

For example, some projects' findings will be a better fit for media coverage, while other projects will serve a less visible audience.

A live presentation offers a chance for interaction and personalization, if you have a skilled presenter following effective practices.[175]

The most comprehensive strategies combine tools and channels. They adapt communications methods and assess what works.

DIGITAL COMMUNICATION

The principles of good communication are the same in the digital and non-digital arenas. Digital communication should be incorporated into the communications plan, not considered separately.

Social media,[176] blogging, webinars, and email offer distinct opportunities and benefit from investment of time, strategy, and skill.

The amount of information on the web increases every hour. Data visualization and processing software make it easier than share data publicly, while publishing tools provide the ability to push content to the Web at the click (or tap) of a button.

Despite the increased ease of sharing information, people's abilities take in information have not changed. For more on the cognitive limits of users, see the chapter on Reporting (Chapter 7). Thus, as an organization trying to get a message across, it is important to work on understanding what information and resources are best shared through a website and other digital formats like social media; how to manage and update the information; and how to share this information in ways that are interesting and useful for user.

WEBSITES

Many projects publish indicators and share information via a website. The design and form of websites change over time, but human behavior remains relatively consistent.

The key to having a website that is used is to take the work out of finding information by eliminating difficult choices, designing pages that are easy to scan, and making it easy for the user to back up and navigate a different path.[178]

Our biggest communications challenge is figuring out what will resonate. When I first started, I'd print out every report. We realized people would look at the handout and throw it away. So, we moved to social media and an e-blast or two every month. We try to produce a community report every month that relates to ACT topics. We promote the reports ourselves, and let people know when a community report card is coming up. We combined a recent report with workshops.

Ann Johnson
ACT Rochester[177]

The web pages for an indicators project are often organized within another website but can also be a standalone site. Standalone sites can be created through free or low-cost, WYSIWYG ("what you see is what you get" – a drag-and-drop tool) platforms. Websites can also be custom-made in-house or by an outside vendor. An indicators project can integrate blogging and other types of software into its website or use the blogging platform as the website (e.g., Tumblr or Medium).

It is worth considering how a skilled contractor (or volunteer) could elevate a project's work by contributing to such areas as branding, graphic design, user experience design, content strategy, or setting up the website itself.

Responsive design and accessibility will make a project's website work for more people. "Responsive" means a website that works on a variety of devices and formats, such as a smartphone and desktop computer. Accessibility means that people with any type of impairment will be able to access and navigate a site. Ideas to make a site accessible include adding alt text to images, making sure forms work with screen readers, and ensuring it is possible to navigate by keyboard alone.

Indicators projects may consider the visibility and accessibility of interactive interfaces in addition to the website overall. A visually appealing, colorful infographic will be of little use to a user with a screen reader (i.e., an assistive technology that enables visually impaired users to still experience the content on the screen by translating the visual material into non-visual media) if there is not another way to access the data. For example, add a textual list of geographies an interactive map; provide links to data sets in accessible formats, like CSV files rather than PDFs. For more information about website accessibility, see the World Wide Web Consortium's (W3C) informational page.[179]

Communications Measurement

Tracking communications is an important way to keep operations nimble and effective. Just like evaluation is an important part of the overall project, data specifically on communications can help a project track successes and identify areas for improvement.

In Chapter 2, we saw how a project can track measures of progress based on process and outcomes. Measures of input and output related to communications can feed into regular project evaluations. Useful communications measures can include:

- Number of website visitors and other web analytics data
- Number of media mentions (e.g., how often was the indicators project mentioned in the news?)
- Number of newsletter or listserv subscribers
- Number of requests for presentations by project representatives
- Number of presentations to community members and decision-makers
- Number of inquiries by email or phone
- Number of social media followers
- Attendance at events

In planning for data collection, think about tracking not only whether indicators have been used, but how they are used.[181] This can include tracking what users do and how often they engage (through clicks, shares, etc.).

My purpose isn't to count clicks or keep people on the website. Our project is a tool to move our community forward.

Ann Johnson
ACT Rochester[180]

However, just because data can be gathered doesn't mean it is always useful to do so. Before instituting a program to track communications measures, ask how knowing a number will affect a project's decision-making about communications or help with the larger effort of evaluating the impact of the indicators project.

Conclusion

While communications is often an afterthought for an indicators project, good communication practices are crucial. Consider writing communications costs into a project budget. Make the case for strong communications to a foundation, business, or community leader. If this isn't possible, seek out specific volunteer support from someone who is skilled in communications. Be flexible and ready to adjust to take advantage of the opportunities present in your external environment – such as a partner planning an event, a fair, or a political process.

Building connections between and within stakeholder groups, and learning responsively with and from the users of the project, will be vital to an indicators project's success. Whether through informal or formal channels, communications will help get the right information to the right people, in a form that makes it likely they will use it for the betterment of their communities.

CHAPTER 11:
COMMUNITY ENGAGEMENT

 Citizens want results they care about, not just data, so citizen priorities should drive what data to collect, report, and use.

Paul Epstein, et al.
Results that Matter[182]

Introduction

Necessarily at the root of community indicators projects are the communities themselves. Here, we use the term "community engagement" (which can also go by the aliases of "citizen participation,"[183] "public engagement," "public participation," and "stakeholder engagement") to apply to the broadest possible community (i.e., the general public, including those who live, work, study or have other connections to the a geography or are connected by an identity or social interactions[184]).

Engaging members of the community is essential to grounding indicators in community priorities and in making them actionable, but it is also challenging and potentially arduous work.[185,186] Community engagement can take place across all kinds of contexts, with many different goals, involving diverse sets of participants.[187] There are many ways to interact with the community, and not all of them reach the point of true engagement. This chapter will present an overview of the concept and offer practical examples from how indicators projects have engaged their communities.

It is important to recognize that community engagement is a process that happens throughout a community indicators project in different forms, playing different roles in different stages. In the early stages of the project, broad community engagement will help ensure that the indicators reflect issues important to the whole community, not just a select few. At other stages of the project, community engagement can happen through smaller committees, including steering committees, technical committees, and action committees. If primary data collection is required, community members may be instrumental in that process. Regardless of the stage, community engagement and communication go hand in hand. Staying informed of new concerns or trends in the community and keeping the community informed of progress, of milestones, of discoveries, is crucial to validating their participation and keeping the work relevant.

Types of engagement

Many frameworks have been put forth to organize the many ways of reaching the public. Several of the most commonly used frameworks[188,189,190,191] for thinking about community engagement are illustrated in Figure 20, below. These conceptual models can be simplified into activities of "transactional," "transitional," and "transformational" engagement. Others have used the terms "communication," "consultation," and "participation" in describing a similar three-tiered classification of modes of engagement.[192]

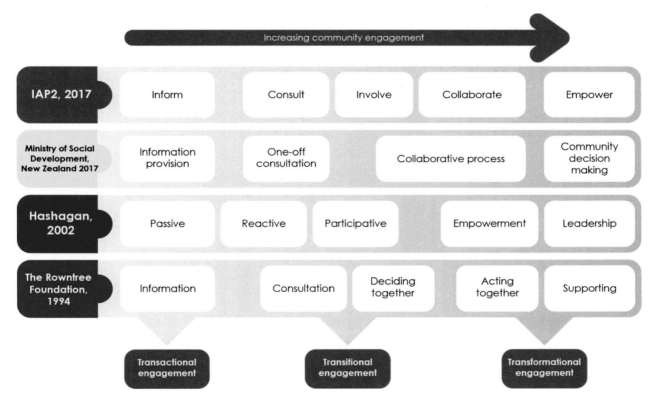

Figure 20: "The continuum of community engagement." Adapted from: Bowen, F., Newenham-Kahindi, A., & Herremans, I. (2010). When Suits Meet Roots: The Antecedents and Consequences of Community Engagement Strategy. Journal of Business Ethics, 95(2), 297–318. https://doi.org/10.1007/s10551-009-0360-1

These frameworks all acknowledge that there are simplistic, **transactional** activities where the flow of information only goes in one direction from the provider of information to the intended audience on the provider's terms. These activities, typically meant to inform, are placed under the umbrella of community engagement, but offer little opportunity for interaction and development.

Transitional processes are more interactive, with opportunities for dialog, joint learning, and leadership by community members.[193] They may involve consultations with the public, efforts to involve the community in decision making within the project, and activities that are truly collaborative within the community (IAP2).[194] Such processes use ongoing dialogues with community members, with an back-and-forth process of learning from one another. This is the minimum level of engagement that community indicators projects should strive to apply.

At the most sophisticated end of the engagement spectrum are the **transformational** engagement activities. Transformational activities are more practical with small groups, given the intense amount of effort they require. These approaches are seen as truly placing the power – typically of decision making– in the hands of the community. In other words, the community is driving the bus, with the project staff there to provide support as needed.

Why engage the community?

Because of the nature and intended use of community indicators, the community should be the driving force behind them (i.e., the foundation on which the project is built and exists). Public input is essential in determining what issues – and thus indicators – are most relevant and important to a community. This knowledge is a key element if the goal of the project is to improve community conditions. Projects that effectively engage with the community will reflect issues that affect and reflect the everyday lives of people of all types. Projects that engage only a handful of (highly involved) stakeholders are at risk of overlooking issues or perspectives that may not be universally known but vitally important to pockets of the community.

Engagement benefits both the indicator project and the community. These benefits include:

- Opportunities for community members (and project leaders) to network with one another; the resulting networks facilitate a flow of information and activity[196,197]
- Opportunities for dialogue. The "transformative power of dialogue" affords people the opportunity to better understand others' views, learn new information, problem solve, and plan for joint action.[198]
- A more informed, aware, and active community. [199]

We just asked questions... it was enlightening to get input from people on what [different topics] meant to them, because our interpretation was totally different.

Karen Hruby
TMT[195]

120

- People having a voice in issues that directly affects their community.
- Approaches that represent broad and diverse interests, rather than those of an elite few.
- Possible mobilization of a powerful grassroots network.[200],[201]
- Increased legitimacy in the community (for the indicators project) when it reflects many voices.[202],[203]
- Building of institutional and political capital and a belief in the productivity of civic engagement, which can facilitate action down the road.[204],[205],[206],[207]

For this to happen, the community should be involved in every step of the indicator process, from conception to dissemination.

Who should be engaged?

Many projects focus their community engagement efforts on leaders within the community. Those people are often more readily identifiable and easier to connect with. While these key stakeholders represent important voices, their voices are ideally not the *only* community voices.

From early discussions of community engagement, there has been an acknowledgement that power and voice are not evenly distributed in communities,[208] and that it is incumbent upon efforts of community engagement to engage those who are traditionally underrepresented. Not only should these groups be engaged, but community engagement activities should be acutely mindful of how racism, privilege, and inequality have shaped the community and the experiences of individuals, and respect the many forms that education, experience, culture, and knowledge can take.[209] This diversity of voices is essential in ensuring that the thoughts and information gathered represent the wide range of experiences had by community members, not just the views of a few dominant stakeholders.[210] In seeking out community members to engage, it is important to include individuals who reflect diversity across characteristics including age, sex, gender identity, race, ethnicity, sexual orientation, employment status, career type, education level, religious affiliation, citizenship status, socioeconomic status, and transportation access/use, among others. This is especially true as the project advances and work groups meet around particular goals/issues/domains to pick the right indicators. Sometimes an issue affects one set of people more strongly than another, so there is a case for expressly striving to have that group or groups represented.

Even if recruitment efforts yield a diverse cohort of participants at the beginning of the project, it is important to periodically step back and assess whether those who are continuing to be actively engaged still reflect a broad-based, diverse group of individuals. The time, involvement, and effort that continued participation can entail may be a bigger barrier to some than to others.

What role will community members play?

From focus groups, to community dinners, to interactive websites, to public hearings, to tele-voting, there are myriad ways and roles to engage the community. Community engagement activities could strive to reach a larger audience for occasional check-ins and a less-intensive activity, or smaller audiences for repeated or more intensive activities, like service on a committee. Community engagement can also be vital in a data-to-action effort, with community members serving as champions for change in areas related to different indicators.

It's kind of a fallacy that we are "dragging people off the street". You take a cross-section of the population and you get a lot of expertise on many different areas. You also get people in the room that can speak their mind.

Noel Gilbrough
Sustainable Calgary[211]

There are five overlapping major roles that individuals from the community can play: **stakeholder** (one who experiences or is otherwise concerned with the community), **advocate** (one encouraging action to benefit the community), **issue framer** (one who makes concerns concrete and known), *evaluator* (of either alternatives or changes over time), and **collaborator** (in making positive change).[212]

In community indicators projects, the same individual may play every one of those roles. In particular, community members are asked to take on the role of issue framers (i.e., those who set the agenda, define the problems to be identified through indicators, and identify solutions).[213]

The metaphor of a camera is used to describe the way the public, as issue framers, will capture the snapshot of the community. As the community members are invited to operate the camera, they are directing what the snapshot will capture. Noted ways of supporting them in this role include involving them from early on in a project to identify and frame the project, promoting dialogs and "deliberative processes" among those engaged, and being flexible and adaptive with regard to

thinking about boundaries, both administrative and geographical.[214] Community members are also likely to serve as **evaluators**, interpreting the information captured by indicators and assessing whether the data represent an improvement over time. Taking this a step further, they may be involved as collaborator in considering both proposed and alternative solutions to problems.

Community Engagement in Action

Approaches used by several successful community indicator projects are included in the boxes below.[215,216,217]

SA2020, San Antonio, TX

SA2020 is a non-profit that arose from a project in 2010 when the mayor launched a community-wide visioning process to help outline priorities for San Antonio.[218]

- Twenty-six community members with diverse interests form a steering committee.

- The project launched a public process for visioning of San Antonio a decade into the future: "What would make San Antonio a world class city, and how would we know if we got there?"

- Input was sought through online surveys, in-person surveys, and five public meetings. This resulted in feedback from about 6000 San Antonians.

- From this feedback, 11 "cause areas" rose to the top. Each cause area had its own vision/goal statements and indicators (59 total indicators then, 61 as of 2018).

- Now that the project is in the indicator tracking stage, they place significant emphasis on story-telling, media, and public relations. Tools include social media accounts, community-wide events, panel discussions, a community blog, e-newsletter, and presentations to community groups

- SA2020 also developed a portal to connect community members with non-profit organizations working to move the needle on indicators.

Magnolia Place Community Initiative (MCI), Los Angeles, CA

MCI is a network of over 70 organizations and resident leaders covering 5 square miles.[219]

- At the beginning of the project, about 30-35 organizations came together to create a "Hope and Dream Statement"

- MCI Neighborhood Ambassadors are a group of about 35 parents who support MCI that originated from a pilot project, "neighbor circles," in which community resident volunteers were trained to host meetings in their homes.

- MCI conducts a community survey every other year, focusing on 23 of the 500 blocks in their catchment area. In 2017, MCI staff and 3 trained residents knocked on 2900 doors and got about 500 responses.

- MCI is training 2 local schools to review data, decide how it should be shared with the community, and identify action steps.

Jacksonville Community Council Inc. (JCCI), Jacksonville, FL

While the original JCCI project no longer exists, it remains a legend in the field of community indicators.[220]

- In the beginning, a volunteer steering committee selected 9 topic areas.

- 100 public volunteers were recruited to serve on 9 task forces, one for each topic. Each task force was given information about what "might and could be measured" and asked to select indicators for their topic area.

- Community members set targets for the indicators that the task forces selected.

- Another committee of citizens served "as evaluators to ensure the emphasis in interpretation and presentation of the report is a citizen emphasis, and the report is kept relevant to the community"[221]

Truckee Meadows Tomorrow (TMT), Reno, NV[222,223]

TMT was born in 1989 from a collaboration between the Economic Development Authority of Western Nevada, Truckee Meadows Regional Planning Agency, Washoe Education Association, and Washoe Medical Center/ now Renown Health. It became an independent nonprofit in 1993.[224]

- Like JCCI, TMT also began with 9 major conceptual areas.

- A task force met with different groups of community members, reaching over 2000 residents. To get the word out about online surveys and events, they partnered with various organizations who had well-read listservs or large e-mail lists.

- TMT provided citizens with possible indicators and had citizens indicate which indicators they feel best addressed the topic. TMT came up with a community engagement process to get feedback on what quality of life meant to different people. From a list that had been made by community members, a broader audience was asked to vote — using Monopoly money— on what issues were most important. Every person got $100 of Monopoly money to allot how they wanted.

- Additionally, to seek as broad-based input as possible, TMT conducted mail and newspaper surveys to try to reach those who had not yet participated. 1100 surveys were collected.

- They also made sure to work with youth groups and "gather information about the thoughts of the future leaders in the community.

- Through the "Adopt an Indicator program," community members (both the general public and those with professional connections to an indicator) adopt one or more indicators to champion.

What challenges could arise?

There are many challenges when translating the theoretical ideals of community engagement into real practices.[225,226] These dilemmas, and potential solutions, include:

Dilemma	Strategies to consider
Scaling up a practice (especially with a focus on face-to-face practices) to large communities.	<ul><li>Focus on smaller units. Think about working with specific neighborhoods, for example.</li><li>Be willing to offer many ways, dates, and times to attend events.</li><li>Reach out to other projects working with a similar sized community to learn about their approaches.</li><li>Consider technologies that might help reach a large number of people in a virtual or digital meeting.</li></ul>
Being inclusive of community members who are often excluded.	<ul><li>Begin by knowing who is in the community – start with demographic data.</li><li>Be proactive in going to them.</li><li>Use existing networks that extend into these pockets of the community to reach out to these community members.</li><li>Honor the many skills, experiences, and insights held by these community members.</li><li>Make sure communications and events are culturally competent.</li></ul>

Navigating tension between the knowledge bases of community members and experts.	• Include both community members and experts together on panels and give them time to engage in dialogue. • Consider using a trained facilitator. • In processes like indicator selection, a weighting system may help balance the needs of the community with the views of the experts in an objective, quantifiable way.
Finding time to properly and thoroughly engage the community.	• Begin the project with the conviction that this is a core element of a community indicators project, and make an explicit commitment to community engagement. • Specify goals for community engagement at the outset of the project. • Develop a community engagement team or task force that can oversee this effort.
Volunteer fatigue.	• Acknowledge, communicate, and celebrate contributions and milestones – even small ones; a sense of progress is important. • Be efficient and punctual in any interactions. • Let volunteers know from the beginning what their expected time commitment will be and honor it. • Seek sources of funding for compensation when possible.

Table 9. Challenges of community engagement and strategies to address them

How can engagement be sustained?

Successful projects have identified some clear strategies for keeping the public engaged.

- Engagement activities must be organized and efficient.[227] This also means that community engagement is strategic. In other words, not every decision requires broad community input (e.g., decisions around webpage platform), and indicator projects should prioritize which activities should be heavily rooted in community engagement.

- The timing, location, and atmosphere of meetings matter as much as the content. Food should be offered as often as possible.

- As the project advances, communicate with participants using the most accessible medium (or multiple media) so they see the products emerging form the efforts.

- Make an interactive product that introduces community members to indicators and lets them explore aspects of their community that they may have been less aware of (see the idea from BNIA below).

- When appropriate, celebrate! Successful indicator projects have made concerted efforts to honor the time and dedication of community members who have played a role.[228] Couple the celebration with a chance to educate more of the community about the indicator project and ways to be involved.

- Form strategic partnerships that foster opportunities to be in regular communication with the community (e.g., with members of the media).

Full circle: Bringing data back to the community

Seema Iyer from BNIA describes some of their tactics for engaging their community and helping the community engage with the data.[229]

"We host Baltimore Data Day every year. We call community-based organizations. It's free and open workshop. We actually call people and register them over the phone to get them to come. … There is hands–on learning, an overview, community members talk about using the data, split into workshops, and demonstrations on how to access data". "Professors said "we need simple pedagogical tools we can plug into our syllabus." We created a learning community on our website. We have 5 modules based on Kids Count in the Classroom and a slew of resources, including teachingwithdata.org." "Every year [after our report comes out] it's an invitation to community-based organizations – we will attend their meetings on their time, because they're already organizing themselves."

CHAPTER 12:
PRACTICAL STRATEGIES FOR COMMUNITY ENGAGEMENT

Introduction

As outlined in the Community Engagement chapter, the heart of any community indicators project is understanding the strengths, needs, and hopes of community members. In most communities, there are some people who are used to having a voice and making their opinions known. It is important that community engagement not be limited to these readily accessible voices. Below are some suggestions for practical ways to engage with community members. Many of these approaches apply whether the goal is to recruit participants for one-time community meetings or focus groups or to be long term volunteers on project committees, but the focus is more on the former. Community Activators provides a guide that offers suggestions more specific to recruitment of long-term volunteers.[230]

Planning for Outreach

For a community indicators project, it is essential that input come from a diverse cross-section of the community; different segments of the community may have unique insights that will go unheard otherwise. Thus, the community engagement process should be conducted mindfully, beginning with an understanding of who is in the community and which community members may need especially purposeful outreach to participate in the process. Soliciting input and volunteers that represent the

Action Plan:

1. Plan timeline and resources for community events
2. Look at demographic data
3. Develop goals for outreach
4. Create a worksheet
5. Reach out to and partner with local organizations
6. Identify logistics related to the community event
7. Identify advertising media and implement
8. Identify best format for invitations and send them
9. Prepare the event

diverse members of the community will likely require thoughtful planning and strategic outreach.

Recruitment Tactics

LOOKING IN MANY PLACES

Community engagement doesn't have to mean ringing every doorbell to meet everyone face to face (although it can!)[231] Rather, most outreach strategies are built on reaching a representative portion of the population that hopefully reflects the whole and who can, as a group, speak to the multitude of issues that are of concern to the community. Reaching the community is integral to the visioning process, but community members should be engaged in other phases of an indicators project, from indicator selection to mobilizing for action. Building this list of diverse voices means recruiting participants from a variety of places.

Begin this planning by looking at demographic data (i.e., census data)[232] to understand the demographic make-up of the community with regard to race and ethnicity, age and income distribution, employment status, occupations, gender, family structure, etc. A worksheet can help organize and plan for outreach.[233] Develop some goals for outreach (e.g., numbers of committees, who is represented on the committees, number of community meetings, etc.).

Partnerships with other local organizations are tremendously helpful in maximizing a project's reach into the community. The following organizations might offer opportunities to connect with a range of community members:[234]

- Housing authorities and groups
- Professional and business associations
- Parent-teacher organizations
- Student government organizations
- Veterans groups
- Social service agencies

- Religious groups
- Hobby and recreational groups
- Volunteer groups
- Cultural organizations
- Neighborhood groups
- Labor union

Comprehensive community engagement should also include the voices of those who may not traditionally be engaged. The groups and organizations listed above are generally comprised of those who are already engaged on some level. However, the leaders of these organizations are often trusted and connected community members who have large networks in the community. One possible strategy is to give such community leaders a significant role in the project, which can include leading recruitment. Beyond official leaders of these groups, key supporters in organizations like these can further outreach to less prominent members of their organizations. For "frequent flyer" volunteers, ask them to bring along a friend, colleague, spouses, parent, or child for a valuable perspective that may not normally be heard. Those organizations can also use their network to advertise your needs or inviting you to recruit members at one of their events

In addition to the above places, other community locations are visited by many community members. These locations may have community bulletin boards, a key staff person who can help spread the word or allow a group to leave flyers or set up an information table.

- Schools (public, private, charter, preschools, K-12, technical, vocational, community colleges, and universities)
- Libraries
- Recreation facilities (parks, pools, gyms, basketball courts, fields, etc.)
- Laundromats

- Post offices
- Grocery stores, corner stores, bodegas
- Medical and veterinary offices
- Barbershops and salons
- Child care centers
- Local sports events (youth and adult)
- Transportation hubs

CONSTRUCTING THE ASK

There are many ways to recruit participants, from flyers, to ads and notices, to social media posts, to in-person invitations, and some are better suited to a given situation than others. Personally extended invitations are often the most impactful, but also the most time consuming.[235] For this, it helps to use any network of supporters that may be available, including contacts or partners at the organizations listed above. An invitation issued by someone with whom the community member can identify, whether with regard to culture, ethnicity, language, gender, etc., may be more likely to yield participation. Provide supporters with a scripted invitation (that they are free to adapt) so the details are clear to everyone and ask them to reach out to their networks with the invitation.

A compelling invitation to participate should:[236,237]

- Be warm and engaging
- Indicate specifically what sort (and duration) of participation is being requested and why it's so important to have the invitee participate
- Point out benefits one receives by participating

In the invitation, it might also help to assure people that they have all the knowledge they need, just as they are. For example, one invitation template reads, "No advanced preparation is necessary. Your own experience is all you need to participate in this meeting."[238]

Once the invitation has been extended, typically a minimum of 3 weeks before the event, reminders sent out close to the event data are also useful in maximizing participation. If possible, leverage the same initial point of contact for extending the reminders. It helps to use an organizational system from the beginning of the invitation process. A spreadsheet or other method of tracking who's should be invited, who was assigned to extend the invitation, who has been invited, who has been reminded, who has RSVP'd, and who attended will make planning for event and future events much easier.

Techniques

The Tamarack Institute provides an index of engagement techniques (along with considerations for each tactic) organized by the 5 levels of engagement outlined by IAP2: inform, consult, involve, collaborate, empower.[239]

Inform	Consult	Involve	Collaborate	Empower
Website	Polls	Crowdsourcing ideas/ideation	Large group meetings	Decision-making Platform
General Information Channels	Voting	Community Mapping	Document co-creating	Citizen Committees
Videos	Surveys	Digital Storytelling	Online Communities	Citizen Juries
Infographics	Interviews	Design Charette	Open Space	Community Indicator Projects
Social Media	Focus Groups	Mind Mapping	Working Groups/Study Circles	Asset-based Community Development (ABCD)
Advertising and Media Coverage	Online Forums	Most Significant Change (MSC)		
Printed Collateral	Online Commenting	Visioning		
Presentations/Live Streaming	Social Media Listening	Scenario Testing		
Expert Panel	Social Media Discussions/Town halls	Citizens' Panels		
Displays/Exhibits	Workshops	Hackathons		
Site visits/Tours	Door-to-door	Participatory Budgeting		
Public Meetings	Kitchen table talks			
	Open houses/pop ups			
	Comment boxes			

Table 10: Example engagement tactics at each of the 5 levels of community engagement. Source: Tamarack Institute. [240]

Some techniques are particularly relevant to exploring different ways of information-gathering and consensus building around actions.

- Visioning is one of the most common methods used at the onset of an effort to maximize community participation and engage it in a creative problem-solving process[241]. By involving the full range of interests and expertise within a given community to envision a desirable future and craft a vision and goals to reach it, this process puts participants in charge of their future and provides a road map to guide them. The goals provide a basis for the selection of domains. A visioning event may be a 4 -6 hour gathering of a representative sample of the community population. Different methods can be used to stimulate conversations and gather input, including versions of Open Space and Conversation Café, or participatory mapping. Results can be collected through technology, dots on board, recording/videotaping.

- Community or participatory mapping[242] is a fun and accessible technique where community members create maps of their community's social, ecological and economic assets, along with historical events of their community. It is useful to address the needs of the community, identify gaps in knowledge, obstacles, strengths or agents of change, and promote ownership in the results while engaging in rich discussion around priorities and issues of concerns. Participatory mapping can be used as part of a visioning event, or to refine the discussion around domains, such as transportation or housing, or to empower participants to envision improvements of their community.

Knock Knock!

If a project decides to go door-to-door to engage community members, particularly in areas where there may be conflict distrust or between residents and authorities, consider these approaches used by **Magnolia Place Community Initiative** in Los Angeles.

- Six weeks before going door-to-door, they worked with partner organizations to distribute flyers that included project information as well as photos of the staff who would be going door to door.

- Staff wore branded shirts to make it clear who they were representing

- MCI trained local residents to conduct the surveys

- A hired Korean-speaking canvasser was able to communicate clearly with the many Korean-speaking families in the area.

Tips for Meetings

Even a great network of volunteers disseminating invitations will yield a low turnout if the events are not convenient to potential participants. When planning the event, whether it's a community forum for hundreds, or a focus group of eight residents, efforts should be made to maximize accessibility, particularly for people whose voices are often less heard in public processes. Below are some suggestions for maximizing participation, with the caveat that it is important to do some legwork to figure out the needs of the specific segment of the community that one is hoping to engage.

Making attendance feasible[243,244,245]

- *Scheduling*
  - Plan for times that are convenient for attendees, whether that's mornings once children are in school, evenings after traditional work hours, or weekends. Ideally, the event would be offered at multiple times to allow for the greatest number of potential participants.
  - Be aware of holidays, both those that might be celebrated in the community, but also those that local schools close for.
  - If you are looking to connect with seniors, be aware that driving after dark may not be desirable.

- See if there are other planned events at an organization where your event could piggyback on attendance. For example, is there a job fair where you could also have a booth soliciting input on your project?
- *Transportation*
  - Aim to hold the event in a place that minimizes transportation time.
  - Ensure that the location is well-served by public transportation and that parking is readily available if people are likely to drive. Consider offering transit fare or parking reimbursements to those who may need them to attend.
  - Consider whether there are ways to offer remote participation if transportation is a major barrier to some who would otherwise be engaged.
- *Location*
  - Many smaller events in local hubs may be more effective in getting a diverse participant base than single large events. To connect with youth, try arranging a visit directly at the school. To connect with seniors, visit senior centers and nursing homes. To connect with parents of young children, work with preschools and daycare centers.
  - Ensure that your event is accessible to those with mobility limitations.
  - Make it easy for late-comers to join the event and be brought up to speed.
- *Awareness of families*
  - In addition to scheduling considerations, provide babysitting or ensure that the event is family friendly and make it clear in the invitation if children are welcome and whether activities will be provided.

Making attendance desirable[246,247]

- *Location*
  - When possible, collaborate with existing community partners to use space that is known and comfortable to community members. This may be a room in a local library, recreation center, WIC office, community space in a housing development, etc.
- *Motivation*
  - People have countless commitments and demands on their time. Some community groups pair their requests for community engagement with activities that make the decision to attend a community engagement event more appealing or practical for community members. For example, co-locating or even co-hosting a job fair, petting zoo, pet vaccination event, health screening, or the like may help draw in people who may not otherwise prioritize attendance at an event for the indicator project.
- *Refreshments*
  - Refreshments help create a welcoming atmosphere and build community. It helps to include the information about refreshments with the invitation. For example, if you are asking people to come after work, knowing that dinner will be provided will help those who otherwise feel a rush to get home to prepare supper.
- *Be mindful of time*

- o   In some communities, this means adhering to the promised schedule. This is especially important if you are asking community members to engage repeatedly. People will be wary of returning if meetings are disorganized or run way over time.
- o   In some communities, it is important that the project organizers consider different cultural concepts of time that may be at play. Rigid adherence to a schedule may make those who come later feel alienated or dissuade them from future participation. One solution could be to hold a reception or meal before the "business" portion of the event, allowing for a window when people can trickle in but still be there for the primary discussion or activity.

Making attendance productive[248]

- *Language access*
  - o   If needed, be sure to have translators/interpreters and materials in different languages available.
  - o   Speak simply. Avoid technical jargon. Limit use of acronyms, and be sure to define acronyms that are used, as well as any other terminology that is important to understanding the issue.
- *Accessibility*
  - o   Ensure that any speaking can be heard throughout the entire space.
  - o   Consider how participants with vision or hearing limitations will be able to participate. Make sure information is available in multiple modes (i.e., visual and oral).
- *Chances for all voices to be heard*
  - o   If planning for a large event, consider how you will ensure that all attendees will feel that this was a productive use of their time and that they had a chance to make their voices heard. Even in smaller groups, some participants may not feel comfortable voicing their thoughts out loud.
  - o   Consider break-out groups.
  - o   Consider individual feedback forms, these could be pen-and-paper, or accessible via smartphone, or, ideally, both.
  - o   Leave participants with a way to reach you in the future, if they think of something else after the event.

Setting the stage for the future

- Offer and/or remind participants of other ways they can be involved in the community indicators project beyond the day's activity, if they are so inspired.
- Be prepared to provide updates back to the community. A key to building a strong indicators project is having an interested, engaged community base, and regular communication helps achieve this.
  - o   Consider collecting contact information so that participants can receive updates about progress throughout the project. Note that in some circumstances, individuals may not wish to provide this information. In such cases, efforts to keep the community informed

134

can focus more on connecting with community organizations and using them as a platform for communication.

APPENDIX A: SOURCES OF DATA FOR COMMUNITY INDICATORS PROJECTS

Some examples of excellent data sources from U.S. federal agencies with data available at small geographies (i.e., county level, city, census track, or ZIP code) include:

- The **U.S. Census Bureau** is the leading source of quality data about the nation's people and economy. It provides data from the Population and Housing Census, Economic Census, Census of Governments, American Community Survey, and many other demographic and economic surveys. www.census.gov
  - The Census Bureau runs the **American FactFinder**, which is the main way to access census data. The website also includes training on how to use this powerful tool to access and download tens of thousands of data tables. www.factfinder.census.gov
- From ecosystem vulnerability to food security to higher education to housing affordability, **Data.gov** contains 14 topic areas, each with many links to data sources of interest. Data.gov provides descriptions of the Federal data sets, information about how to access the data sets, and tools that leverage government data sets. www.data.gov
- The **Centers for Disease Control and Prevention (CDC)** provide multiple data hubs.
  - The **Data and Statistics** page includes numerous tools grouped by topic that provide access to credible, reliable health data and statistics. Note that these data are often available at the state or national level, but can be harder to find at smaller geographies. www.cdc.gov/DataStatistics
  - **CDC WONDER** is short for Wide-ranging OnLine Data for Epidemiologic Research. It offers public-use data sets about mortality, natality and the incidence and rates of many diseases and illnesses as well as other topics . http://wonder.cdc.gov
  - **Youth Risk Behavior Surveillance System (YRBSS)** monitors six types of health-risk behaviors that contribute to the leading causes of death and disability among youth and adults. www.cdc.gov/healthyyouth/data/yrbs/index.htm
- The **Health Resources and Administration (HRSA)** Data Warehouse provides a single point of access to resources, and demographic data for reporting on HRSA activities with focuses on uninsured, underserved, and special needs populations. https://datawarehouse.hrsa.gov/
- The **Bureau of Justice Statistics** publishes data on crime, criminal offenders, victims of crime, and the operation of justice systems at all levels of government. http://bjs.ojp.usdoj.gov/
- The **Bureau of Labor Statistics (BLS),** through their **Local Area Unemployment Statistics** publishes data on the labor force size, unemployment rate, and number of individuals employed/unemployed for most states, counties, and cities. http://data.bls.gov/cgi-bin/dsrv?la

- The **Home Mortgage Disclosure Act (HMDA)** offers access to lending institutions public loan data. www.ffiec.gov/hmda/default.htm
- The **National Center for Educational Statistics (NCES)** is the primary federal entity for collecting and analyzing data related to education. www.nces.ed.gov
- The **U.S. Department of Agriculture (USDA) Food Environment Atlas** provides a spatial overview of food environment factors, such as store/restaurant proximity, food prices, food and nutrition assistance programs, and community characteristics. www.ers.usda.gov/FoodAtlas/www.ers.usda.gov/FoodAtlas/
- The **U.S. Environmental Protection Agency** offers data on drinking water. www.epa.gov/waterdata/drinking-water-toolswww.epa.gov/waterdata/drinking-water-tools
- The **Department of Housing and Urban** Development (HUD) releases annual reports on the homeless populations in county and state geographies. www.hudexchange.info/programs/coc/coc-homeless-populations-and-subpopulations-reports/www.hudexchange.info/programs/coc/coc-homeless-populations-and-subpopulations-reports/
  - **HUD USER** provides access to the **American Housing Survey**, HUD median family income limits, as well as microdata from research initiatives on topics such as housing discrimination, the HUD-insured multifamily housing stock, and the public housing population. www.huduser.gov

In addition to those federal resources, a number of interest groups offer free data access to specialized databases:

- **Community Commons** offers community-level data and maps on various topics related to equity, the economy, education, food health and the environment. www.communitycommons.org/maps-data/
- **Kids Count Data Center** is an expansive source of data on children and families. http://datacenter.kidscount.org/
- The annual **County Health Rankings** measure vital health factors, including high school graduation rates, obesity, smoking, unemployment, access to healthy foods, the quality of air and water, income inequality, and teen births in nearly every county in America. www.countyhealthrankings.org/
- The **National Association of Realtors (NAR)** has a website for each state's association of Realtors which will often publish reports on housing values and sometimes release the underlying data sets. Additionally, NAR lists median home price data available by metropolitan area. www.realtor.org/topics/metropolitan-median-area-prices-and-affordability/data
- **Feeding America** is the nation's largest domestic hunger-relief organization. In addition their reports on food insecurity in particular populations (rural, children, elderly, etc.), there is an interactive tool for exploring data from Feeding America's annual Map the Meal Gap project. http://map.feedingamerica.org/

- The **Dartmouth Atlas of Health Care** uses Medicare data to provide information and analysis about national, regional, and local markets, as well as hospitals and their affiliated physicians. www.dartmouthatlas.org/
- The **National Equity Atlas** offers an interactive tool for generating graphics at the state, regional, or city level around a number of diverse indicators. Data is split out by racial/ethnic groups to highlight equity issues. http://nationalequityatlas.org/indicators
- The **Hispanic Research Center** offers several data tools related to children and family and economic indicators. www.hispanicresearchcenter.org/resources/interactive-data-tools/

Finally, here are a few pages that actively compile data sources and may include links to more specialized data for your project or region or new sources that have emerged since the time of this publication.

- **Partners in Information Access for the Public Health Workforce** is a collaboration of U.S. government agencies, public health organizations, and health sciences libraries which provides timely, convenient access to selected public health resources on the Internet. Their page includes links for databases in different states as well as the United States as a whole. https://phpartners.org/health_stats.html

- **State of the Cities Data Systems** (SOCDS) The SOCDS provides data for individual Metropolitan Areas, Central Cities, and Suburbs. www.huduser.gov/portal/datasets/socds.html

- The **Institute for Research on Poverty** has compiled a list of websites, arranged by topic in alphabetical order, where data on topics ranging from WIC and TANF to health and child wellbeing may be accessed. https://www.irp.wisc.edu/faqs/faq6.htm

APPENDIX B: ADDITIONAL RESOURCES TO MOVE FROM DATA TO ACTION

Some communities are brimming with ideas on how to make improvements. Others may need help deciding what could be possible or how best to proceed. The following is a (by no means comprehensive) list of resources that offer ideas for practices, programs, and policies that can affect change in many areas important to communities.

Support for Policies

- ChangeLab offers guidance and resources on ways to implement policy, systems, and environmental (PSE) changes on many topics including healthy housing, active communities, and food systems. http://www.changelabsolutions.org/healthy-planning
- This webinar, also from Changelab, provides an introduction to best practices on how to implement PSE approaches, including case studies. http://www.changelabsolutions.org/publications/pse-101-building-healthier-communities
- This toolkit from Community Tool Box provides guidance for bringing about policy change in organizations and communities: http://ctb.ku.edu/en/influencing-policy-development

Ideas for Programs and Practices

- The Community Tool Box provides materials for learning about collective impact[249] as well as tips for facilitating the brainstorming process[250]
- The What Works Clearinghouse (WWC) offers strategies that have been successful in education. https://ies.ed.gov/ncee/wwc/
- The Rural Health Information Hub offers toolkits on topics ranging from services integration, to rural transportation, to community health workers (*promotoras*) and more. https://www.ruralhealthinfo.org/community-health/toolkits
- What Works for Health provides information to help select and implement evidence-informed policies, programs, and system changes that will improve a variety of health-related factors. http://www.countyhealthrankings.org/roadmaps/what-works-for-health
- This database of best practices from the Community Tool Box has numerous suggestions, sorted by topic area. http://ctb.ku.edu/en/databases-best-practices
- A model and a set of guidelines from the RAND Corporation focuses on building participation in the arts. https://www.rand.org/pubs/monograph_reports/MR1323.html
- This page from the New York State Department of Health lists many examples and strategies for dealing with everything from air pollutants to water quality to violence. https://www.health.ny.gov/prevention/prevention_agenda/2013-2017/plan/healthy_environment/ebi/index.htm
- The Annie E. Casey Foundation offers guidance on topics ranging from child welfare to economic opportunity to juvenile justice. http://www.aecf.org/work/community-change/
- Blueprints lists evidence-based programs promoting youth development. http://www.blueprintsprograms.com/programs

APPENDIX C: FACTORS INFLUENCING THE SUCCESS OF COLLABORATION

From: Mattessich, P. (2001). Collaboration: What Makes It Work, 2nd Edition: A Review of Research Literature on Factors Influencing Successful Collaboration. Amherst H. Wilder Foundation.

1. Factors Related to the ENVIRONMENT

A. History of collaboration or cooperation in the community

A history of collaboration or cooperation exists in the community and offers the potential collaborative partners an understanding of the roles and expectations required in collaboration and enables them to trust the process.

B. Collaborative group seen as a legitimate leader in the community

The collaborative group (and, by implication, the agencies in the group) is perceived within the community as reliable and competent—at least related to the goals and activities it intends to accomplish.

C. Favorable political and social climate

Political leaders, opinion-makers, persons who control resources, and the public support (or at least do not oppose) the mission of the collaborative group.

2. Factors Related to MEMBERSHIP CHARACTERISTICS

A. Mutual respect, understanding, and trust

Members of the collaborative group share an understanding and respect for each other and their respective organizations: how they operate, their cultural norms and values, their limitations, and their expectations.

B. Appropriate cross section of members

The collaborative group includes representatives from each segment of the community who will be affected by its activities. It engages members at the appropriate time and at an appropriate level of involvement.

C. Members see collaboration as in their self-interest

Collaborating partners believe that they will benefit from their involvement in the collaboration and that the advantages of membership will offset costs such as slower decision making processes.

D. Ability to compromise

Collaborating partners are able to compromise, since the many decisions within a collaborative effort cannot possibly fit the preferences of every member perfectly.

3. Factors Related to PROCESS AND STRUCTURE

A. Members share a stake in both process and outcome

Members of a collaborative group feel "ownership" of both the way the group works and the results or products of its work.

B. Multiple layers of participation

Every level (upper management, middle management, front line) within each partner organization has involvement in the collaborative initiative. Each layer brings different assets to the collaboration and may need to be involved to different degrees and at different stages of development.

C. Flexibility

The collaborative group remains open to varied ways of shifting its internal structure, organizing itself, and performing activities to accomplish its work.

D. Development of clear roles and guidelines

The collaborating partners jointly develop a set of shared operating principles. They clearly understand their roles and responsibilities and are committed to carrying them out.

E. Adaptability to changing conditions

The collaborative group has the ability to make changes, even to major goals, members, etc., in order to deal with changing conditions in the external environment.

F. Appropriate pace of development

The structure, resources, and activities of the collaborative group change over time to meet the needs of the collaborative group without overwhelming its capacity, at each point throughout the initiative.

4. Factors Related to COMMUNICATION

A. Open and frequent communication

Collaborative group members interact often, update one another, discuss issues openly, create transparency, and convey all necessary information to one another and to people outside of the group.

B. Established informal relationships and communication links

In addition to formal channels of communication, members establish personal connections—producing a better, more informed, and cohesive group.

5. Factors Related to PURPOSE

A. Concrete, attainable goals and objectives

Goals and objectives of the collaborative group are clear to all partners, and can realistically be attained.

B. Shared vision

Collaborating partners have the same vision, with clearly agreed-upon mission, operating principles, objectives, and strategy. The shared vision may exist at the outset of collaboration, or the partners may develop a vision as they work together.

C. Unique purpose

The mission and goals, or approach, of the collaborative group differ, at least in part, from the mission and goals, or approach, of the member organizations.

6. Factors Related to RESOURCES

A. Sufficient funds, staff, materials, and time

The collaborative group has an adequate, consistent financial base, along with the staff and materials needed to support its operations. It allows sufficient time to achieve its goals and includes time to nurture the collaboration.

B. Skilled leadership

The individual who provides leadership for the collaborative group has organizing, facilitation, and interpersonal skills, such as emotional intelligence and cultural competence, and carries out the role with fairness. Thus, the leader is granted respect or "legitimacy" by the collaborative partners.

APPENDIX D: COMMUNITY INDICATORS-PERFORMANCE MEASURES (CI-PM) INTEGRATION DESCRIPTIVE (MATURITY) MODEL

	Separate CI & PM projects	Stage 2	Stage 3	Mature integration CI-PM
What	**Community Indicators (CI)**			Citizen-driven CI's determine PM impacts linked to quantifiable & measurable results: community needs, sustainability, resource allocation, data-driven policy decisions, & next steps for decision options and priorities
	Metrics quantifying values, community, conditions, outcomes & results important to wide-ranging residents within a community	Visioning process involving citizens, key stakeholders, and governmental and nongovernmental entities	Metrics focus on community and programmatic outcomes involving decision- and policy-makers through consensus-building	
	Performance Measures (PM)			
	Metrics documenting the outputs of services provided by a government or nongovernmental entity	Linkages between strategic and annual performance planning with metrics documenting the outputs and outcomes of services provided by a government or nongovernmental entity	Citizens and other key community stakeholders participate in the development of output and outcome metrics through forums, feedback systems, or advisory bodies	
Why	**Community Indicators (CI)**			Transparent results-based governance & decision making consistent with citizen priorities for positive community change, community capacity building, economic development & land use, sustainability, reporting for citizen accountability & civic trust
	Knowledge-producing story of where a community is today, in relation to where it's come from	Evidence of citizen priorities as reflected by indictors through credible and reliable data that stimulate public dialogue and debate	Evaluation and public debate determine the whys of community conditions, strategies developed and implemented, and resources identified and committed to improve community conditions	
	Performance Measures (PM)			
	Knowledge-producing managerial performance system to achieve efficiencies and improve costs in relation to programs and departments/ divisions/ agencies	Improved data and performance-based budgeting and resource allocation through credible and reliable data. More effective service delivery ROI to citizens in allocating limited resources at all levels demonstrated	Outcomes of programs and services demonstrated that reflect citizens and other key stakeholders' priorities	

	Separate CI & PM projects	Stage 2	Stage 3	Mature integration CI-PM
When	**Community Indicators (CI)**			
	Historical measures and trends over time alerting the need for improvement	Leading and lagging indicators benchmarked for measurable improvement or decline	Long-term and annual goals and targets established periodically and progress measured and publicly reported	Evidence on demand – knowing where residents get their information, what their priorities are & what info they want to know about – within defined time periods, used for regular tracking & strategic decision making
	Performance Measures (PM)			
	Annual performance measures	Annual measures progress linked to annual budget development and decisions	Strategic and annual performance goals influence budget discussions and decisions. Community indicators influence the strategic and annual performance goals. Strategic and annual performance goals' progress publicly reported	
Where	**Community Indicators (CI)**			
	Defined community area	Regional and intergovernmental collaboration and comparisons	Defined community area, demographic groups, neighborhoods and street-level data or larger state and neighboring/regional areas crossing political boundaries. Compared to other defined areas, as appropriate	Localized neighborhoods to any defined group within a geographic area, regardless of political boundaries
	Performance Measures (PM)			
	Local government departments/divisions within a defined geopolitical boundary	Contributions of programs and services to changes in community conditions identified along with those of	Regional and intergovernmental collaboration and comparisons	

	Separate CI & PM projects	Stage 2	Stage 3	Mature integration CI-PM
		other public agencies, nongovernmental entities, and businesses		
Who	**Community Indicators (CI)**			Committed accountability for improvements & collaborative advocacy, inputs & use (diverse government, public/citizen, nonprofit & business engagement & participation at all stages) as leadership changes over time
	Community residents likely to control or influence community conditions	Key community stakeholders from all sectors (diverse institutional and business leaders, civic and community groups, local government, policy- and decisionmakers) likely to control or influence community conditions	Coalitions, networks, compacts and other community organizing efforts form to lead community change	
	Performance Measures (PM)			
	Government entity management	Policy-makers and elected officials	Networks of community stakeholders including government and nongovernment entities, legislative bodies, regional partners, and coalitions	

TABLE OF FIGURES

TABLE OF TABLES

Index

ACKNOWLEDGMENTS

This work was supported by the William K. Kellogg Foundation and we are very grateful for their focus on communities and data.

We also thank the following individuals/organization for sharing their knowledge and providing quotes and examples to support this narrative:

- Susan Cohn, previously with Jacksonville Community Council, Inc.
- Molly Cox, SA2020
- Craig Helmstetter, previously with Minnesota Compass
- Karen Hruby, Truckee Meadows Tomorrow
- Seema Iyer, Baltimore Neighborhood Indicators Alliance
- Ann Johnson, ACT Rochester
- Sam Joo, Magnolia Place Community Initiative
- Noel Keough, Sustainable Calgary
- Allison Liuzzi, Minnesota Compass
- Paul Mattessich, Wilder Research
- Kathy Pettit, NNIP
- Frank Ridzi, CNY Vitals

This book was authored by Chantal Stevens, Madeleine deBlois, Ruth Hamberg and Joe Baldwin.

WORKS CITED

[1] History of the Russell Sage Foundation. Russell Sage Foundation. Retrieved 10 October 2018.

[2] Community Indicators Consortium. (2018). Indicator Projects. Retrieved February 16, 2018, from http://communityindicators.net/indicator-projects/

[3] Johnson, Ann. Better Know a Community Indicators Project Webinar: ACT Rochester (May 22, 2015) Retrieved 2/3/2018 from http://communityindicators.net/knowledge/better-know-a-community-indicators-project-webinar-recordings/

[4] Jones, Patrick. Better Know a Community Indicators Project Webinar: Community Indicators Initiative of Spokane (January 30, 2015) Retrieved 2/3/2018 from http://communityindicators.net/knowledge/better-know-a-community-indicators-project-webinar-recordings/

[5] Harris, Jesse. Better Know a Community Indicators Project Webinar: Capital Region Collaborative's Community Indicators Project (2018-03-30) Retrieved 5/3/2018 from http://communityindicators.net/knowledge/better-know-a-community-indicators-project-webinar-recordings/

[6] Innes, Judith E. and David E. Booher (2000)., Indicators for Sustainable Communities: A Strategy Building on Complexity Theory and Distributed Intelligence Planning Theory & Practice,Vol.1,No.2

[7] Barrington-Leigh, C., & Escande, A. (2018). Measuring Progress and Well-Being: A Comparative Review of Indicators. Social Indicators Research, 135(3), 893–925. https://doi.org/10.1007/s11205-016-1505-0

[8] Jones, Patrick. Better Know a Community Indicators Project Webinar: Community Indicators Initiative of Spokane (2015-01-30) Retrieved 2/3/2018 from http://communityindicators.net/knowledge/better-know-a-community-indicators-project-webinar-recordings/

[9] International Association for Public Participation (IAP2). (October 21, 2013). IAP2's Public Participation Spectrum. Retrieved from https://c.ymcdn.com/sites/www.iap2.org/resource/resmgr/foundations_course/IAP2_P2_Spectrum_FINAL.pdf?hhSearchTerms=%22spectrum%22

[10] Smolko, R., Strange, C. J., & Venetoulis, J. (2006). The Community Indicators Handbook: Measuring Progress Toward Healthy and Sustainable Communities (2nd ed.) (pp.27). San Francisco, CA: Redefining Progress.

[11] National Association of County and City Health Officials. (2018). Phase 2: Visioning. Retrieved February 17, 2018, from https://www.naccho.org/programs/public-health-infrastructure/performance-improvement/community-health-assessment/mapp/phase-2-visioning

[12] Green, G., Haines, A., & Halebsky, S. (2000). Building our future - A Guide to Community visioning. Cooperative Extension of the University of Wisconsin. Retrieved from https://learningstore.uwex.edu/Assets/pdfs/G3708.pdf

[13] Community Tool Box. (2018). MAPP: Mobilizing for Action through Planning and Partnerships. Retrieved April 17, 2018, from https://ctb.ku.edu/en/table-of-contents/overview/models-for-community-health-and-development/mapp/main

[14] Flora, C., J. Flora, S. Fey. (2004). Rural Communities: Legacy and Change (2nd Edition). Boulder Colo: Westview Press.

[15] Canadian Index of Wellbeing. (2012). Domains and indicators. Retrieved February 16, 2018, from https://uwaterloo.ca/canadian-index-wellbeing/what-we-do/domains-and-indicators

[16] United Nations. (n.d.). Sustainable development goals. Retrieved January 16, 2018, from http://www.un.org/sustainabledevelopment/sustainable-development-goals/

[17] U.S. Department of Health and Human Services. (2018). Social Determinants of Health. Retrieved March 16, 2018, from https://www.healthypeople.gov/2020/topics-objectives/topic/social-determinants-of-health

[18] Jones, Patrick, Better Know a Community Indicators Project Webinar: Community Indicators Initiative of Spokane (January 30, 2015) Retrieved 2/3/2018 from http://communityindicators.net/knowledge/better-know-a-community-indicators-project-webinar-recordings/

[19] Cohn, Susan. Better Know a CI Project Webinar: Jacksonville's Community Indicators (February 27, 2015) Retrieved 2/3/2018 from http://communityindicators.net/knowledge/better-know-a-community-indicators-project-webinar-recordings/

[20] W.K. Kellogg Foundation. (2017). Step-by-Step Guide to Evaluation. Retrieved March 16, 2018, from https://www.wkkf.org:443/resource-directory/resource/2010/w-k-kellogg-foundation-evaluation-handbook

[21] Macdonald, B., Rust, C., Thrift, C., & Swanson, D. (2012). Measuring the Performance and Impact of Community Indicators Systems: Insights on frameworks and examples of key performance indicators. International Institute for Sustainable Development. Retrieved from https://www.iisd.org/sites/default/files/publications/measuring_performance_communtiy_indicators.pdf

[22] Harris, Jesse. Better Know a Community Indicators Project Webinar: Capital Region Collaborative's Community Indicators Project (2018-03-30) Retrieved 5/3/2018 from http://communityindicators.net/knowledge/better-know-a-community-indicators-project-webinar-recordings/

[23] Kania, J., & Kramer, M. (2011). Collective Impact. Stanford Social Innovation Review, Winter 2011. Retrieved from http://c.ymcdn.com/sites/www.lano.org/resource/dynamic/blogs/20131007_093137_25993.pdf

[24] Cohn, Susan. Better Know a CI Project Webinar: Jacksonville's Community Indicators (February 27, 2015) Retrieved 2/3/2018 from http://communityindicators.net/knowledge/better-know-a-community-indicators-project-webinar-recordings/

[25] Luetke, Michelle (2018). 2018-02-02. Better Know a Community Indicators Project CIC webinar: Santa Cruz County Community Assessment Project. Retrieved 2/3/2018 from http://communityindicators.net/knowledge/better-know-a-community-indicators-project-webinar-recordings/

[26] Ibid.

[27] MacDonald, G. (n.d.). Criteria for Selection of High-Performing Indicators (Evaluation Checklists Project). Retrieved from https://www.wmich.edu/sites/default/files/attachments/u350/2014/Indicator_checklist.pdf

[28] Briggs, D., Corvalan, C., & Nurminen, M. (n.d.). Development of Environmental Health Indicators. In Linkage Methods for Environment and Health Analysis: General guidelines. World Health Organization. Retrieved from http://apps.who.int/iris/bitstream/10665/62988/1/WHO_EHG_95.26_eng.pdf

[29] Briggs, D. (2003). Making a difference: Indicators to improve children's environmental health. Geneva: World Health Organization. Retrieved from http://www.who.int/phe/children/childrenindicators/en/

[30] Intergovernmental Task Force on Monitoring Water Quality, Interagency Advisory Committee on Water Data, & Water Information Coordination Program. (1995). Appendix E -- Indicator-Selection Criteria (The Nationwide Strategy for Improving Water-Quality Monitoring In The United States). Washington, DC: U.S. Geological Survey. Retrieved from https://acwi.gov/appendixes/AppendE.html

[31] Brown, D. (2009). Good Practice Guidelines for Indicator Development and Reporting. Presented at the Third World Forum on 'Statistics, Knowledge and Policy' Charting Progress, Building Visions, Improving Life, Busan, Korea. Retrieved from https://www.oecd.org/site/progresskorea/43586563.pdf

[32] von Schirnding, Y. (2002). Health in Sustainable Development Planning: The role of indicators. World Health Organization. Retrieved from http://www.who.int/wssd/resources/indicators/en/

[33] Strive Partnership. (2013, March). Developing Shared Measures: Lessons Learned from Collective Impact Efforts in Greater Cincinnati. PowerPoint. Retrieved from http://www.collaborationforimpact.com/wp-content/uploads/2014/01/Developing_Shared_Measures_Lessons-Learned.pdf

[34] FSG & Community Center for Education Results. (2013). Instructions for Developing Shared Metrics. Retrieved from https://collectiveimpactforum.org/resources/working-group-instructions-developing-shared-metrics

[35] United Nations Environment Program. (n.d.). An overview of environmental indicators ; state of the art and perspectives. Retrieved November 2, 2017, from http://www.rivm.nl/dsresource?objectid=13cfdc30-b375-4c5c-a967-e8f62a70bdc5&type=org&disposition=inline

[36] Smolko, R., Strange, C. J., & Venetoulis, J. (2006). The Community Indicators Handbook: Measuring Progress Toward Healthy and Sustainable Communities (2nd ed.). San Francisco, CA: Redefining Progress.

[37] Ibid.

[38] MacDonald, G. (n.d.). Criteria for Selection of High-Performing Indicators (Evaluation Checklists Project). Retrieved from https://www.wmich.edu/sites/default/files/attachments/u350/2014/Indicator_checklist.pdf

[39] National Center for HIV/AIDS, Viral Hepatitis, STD, and TB Prevention. (n.d.). Identifying the Components of a Logic Model. Retrieved March 18, 2018, from https://www.cdc.gov/std/Program/pupestd/Components%20of%20a%20Logic%20Model.pdf

[40] Smolko, R., Strange, C. J., & Venetoulis, J. (2006). The Community Indicators Handbook: Measuring Progress Toward Healthy and Sustainable Communities (2nd ed.). San Francisco, CA: Redefining Progress.

41 Ridzi, Frank. Vice President, Community Investment. Central New York Community Foundation. (February 2, 2018). Telephone interview.

42 Institute for Advanced Culture and Studies, University of Virginia. (2018). Indicator Explorer • Thriving Cities. Retrieved March 18, 2018, from http://explore.thrivingcities.com/indicators

[43] Iyer, Seema, Associate Director, Jacob France Institute; Director, Baltimore Neighborhood Indicators Alliance. (January 31, 2018). Telephone interview.

[44] Iyer, Seema, Associate Director, Jacob France Institute; Director, Baltimore Neighborhood Indicators Alliance. (January 31, 2018). Telephone interview.

[45] Healthy People 2020. (n.d.). Retrieved December 1, 2017, from https://www.healthypeople.gov

[46] United Nations. (n.d.). Sustainable development goals. Retrieved February 16, 2018, from http://www.un.org/sustainabledevelopment/sustainable-development-goals/

[47] Vision Zero Network | Making our streets safer. (2017). Retrieved March 1, 2018, from https://visionzeronetwork.org/

[48] U.S. Department of Health and Human Services. (2018). Maternal, Infant, and Child Health | Healthy People 2020. Retrieved March 18, 2018, from https://www.healthypeople.gov/2020/topics-objectives/topic/maternal-infant-and-child-health/objectives

[49] Baltimore Neighborhood Indicators Alliance. (2014). BNIA – Baltimore Neighborhood Indicators Alliance. Retrieved March 18, 2018, from https://bniajfi.org/vital_signs/

[50] Center for Governmental Research, Inc. (2018). ACT Rochester | Community Indicators for the Greater Rochester Area. Retrieved March 18, 2018, from http://www.actrochester.org/

[51] Centers for Disease Control and Promotion. (2018). Behavioral Risk Factors: Selected Metropolitan Area Risk Trends (SMART) MMSA Prevalence Data (2011 to Present). Retrieved March 18, 2018, from https://chronicdata.cdc.gov/Behavioral-Risk-Factors/Behavioral-Risk-Factors-Selected-Metropolitan-Area/j32a-sa6u

[52] Pencheon, D. (2008). The Good Indicators Guide: Understanding how to use and choose indicators. Retrieved from http://webarchive.nationalarchives.gov.uk/20100415155746/http://www.eac.cpft.nhs.uk/viewResource.aspx?id=17235&sUri=http%3a%2f%2fwww.erpho.org.uk%2f

[53] Statistics Canada. (2017, June 16). Use of administrative data. Retrieved March 30, 2018, from http://www.statcan.gc.ca/pub/12-539-x/2009001/administrative-administratives-eng.htm

[54] https://www.library.pitt.edu/subject_specialists

[55] Iyer, Seema, Associate Director, Jacob France Institute; Director, Baltimore Neighborhood Indicators Alliance. (January 31, 2018). Telephone interview.

[56] Iyer, Seema, Associate Director, Jacob France Institute; Director, Baltimore Neighborhood Indicators Alliance. (January 31, 2018). Telephone interview.

[57] U.S. Census Bureau. (n.d.). Decennial Census of Population and Housing. Retrieved February 12, 2018, from https://www.census.gov/programs-surveys/decennial-census.html

[58] U.S. Census Bureau. (n.d.). About the Survey. Retrieved March 19, 2018, from https://www.census.gov/programs-surveys/acs/about.html

[59] U.S. Census Bureau. (n.d.). Confidence interval (American Community Survey). Retrieved March 30, 2018, from https://factfinder.census.gov/help/en/confidence_interval_american_community_survey.htm

[60] U.S. Census Bureau. (n.d.). 2012-2016 American Community Survey 5-Year Estimates, Table DP05 - ACS Demographic and Housing Estimates. Retrieved March 30, 2018, from https://factfinder.census.gov/faces/tableservices/jsf/pages/productview.xhtml?src=CF

[61] Pencheon, D. (2008). The Good Indicators Guide: Understanding how to use and choose indicators. Conventry, UK: NHS Institute for Innovation and Improvement. Retrieved from https://fingertips.phe.org.uk/documents/The%20Good%20Indicators%20Guide.pdf

[62] Mattessich, Paul. Executive Director, Wilder Research. (February 5, 2018). Telephone Interview.

[63] Liuzzi, Allison. Project Director. Minnesota Compass. (January 24, 2018). Telephone interview.

[64] Annie E. Casey Foundation. (2018.). KIDS COUNT Data Books. Retrieved April 19, 2018, from http://www.aecf.org/

[65] Cox, Molly. (2016-06-04) Better Know a Community Indicators Project Webinar: San Antonio SA2020. Retrieved 2/3/2018 from http://communityindicators.net/knowledge/better-know-a-community-indicators-project-webinar-recordings/

[66] Johnson, Ann. Director, ACT Rochester. (January 30, 2018). Telephone interview.

[67] Ibid

[68] Minnesota Compass (2018). Accessed March 2018. www.mncompass.org.

[69] Iyer, Seema, Associate Director, Jacob France Institute; Director, Baltimore Neighborhood Indicators Alliance. (January 31, 2018). Telephone interview.

[70] Comparison Dashboard. Coastal Georgia Indicators Coalition. Accessed February 2018 http://www.coastalgaindicators.org/indicators/index/dashboard?alias=comparison

[71] Tableau Public. https://public.tableau.com/en-us/s/

[72] Pettit, Kathy. Director of the National Neighborhood Indicators Partnership, The Urban Institute. (January 31, 2018). Telephone interview.

[73] Hruby, Karen Hruby. Past Executive Director, Truckee Meadow Tomorrow. (February 9, 2018). Telephone interview.

[74] National Cancer Institute. Making Data Talk: Communicating Public Health Data to the Public, Policy Makers, and the Press (2011). National Institute of Health. https://www.cancer.gov/publications/health-communication

[75] National Cancer Institute. Making Data Talk: Communicating Public Health Data to the Public, Policy Makers, and the Press (2011). National Institute of Health. https://www.cancer.gov/publications/health-communication

[76] Pinnacle Public Relations (2009). Communications Guidebook. Central Europe Programme – Cooperating for Success.

[77] Conscious Style Guide (2018). Conscious Style Guide: About. Accessed December 2017 http://consciousstyleguide.com/about

[78] Linguistic Society of America (2016). Guidelines for Inclusive Language. Accessed October 2017 https://www.linguisticsociety.org/content/guidelines-inclusive-language

[79] Chicago Manual (2016). Sarah Grey Talks about Inclusive Language. CMOS Shop Talk. Accessed October 2017 http://cmosshoptalk.com/2016/09/13/sarah-grey-talks-about-inclusive-language

[80] VanDeCarr, P. (2015). 3 Tips for Telling Stories That Move People to Action. The Chronicle of Philanthropy. https://www.philanthropy.com/article/3-Tips-for-Telling-Stories/228559

[81] Lavis, J., Robertson, D., Woodside, J., McLeod, C., and Abelson, J. (2003). How Can Research Organizations More Effectively Transfer Research Knowledge to Decision Makers? The Milbank Quarterly 81:2. https://www.ncbi.nlm.nih.gov/pmc/articles/PMC2690219

[82] Health, C. (2007). Made to Stick: Why Some Ideas Survive and Others Die. Random House: United States.

[83] Northside Funders Group. North@Work. Accessed February 2018 http://northsidefunders.org/approach/northwork

[84] FrameWorks Institute. The Wide Angle Lens: Telling Thematic Stories for Social Change. Accessed October 2018 http://www.frameworksinstitute.org/workshops/wideanglelens/children/intro.html

[85] Iyer, Seema, Associate Director, Jacob France Institute; Director, Baltimore Neighborhood Indicators Alliance. (January 31, 2018). Telephone interview.

[86] Johnson, Ann. Director, ACT Rochester. (January 30, 2018). Telephone interview.

[87] Bailey, T. J. (2004, March). "Advances in the Science and Practice of Community Indicators" Opening Plenary Remarks. Presented at the Community Quality of Life Conference, Reno, NV. Retrieved from https://www.neighborhoodindicators.org/sites/default/files/publications/reno_plenary.pdf

[88] American Planning Association. (n.d.). » Policy, Systems and Environmental Change Strategies. Retrieved October 23, 2017, from http://plan4health.us/policy-systems-and-environmental-change-strategies/

[89] Community Tool Box. (2017). MAPP: Mobilizing for Action through Planning and Partnerships. Center for Community Health and Development at the University of Kansas. Retrieved from http://ctb.ku.edu/en/table-of-contents/overview/models-for-community-health-and-development/mapp/main

[90] Bailey, T. J. (2004, March). "Advances in the Science and Practice of Community Indicators" Opening Plenary Remarks. Presented at the Community Quality of Life Conference, Reno, NV. Retrieved from https://www.neighborhoodindicators.org/sites/default/files/publications/reno_plenary.pdf

[91] Smolko, R., Strange, C. J., & Venetoulis, J. (2006). The Community Indicators Handbook: Measuring Progress Toward Healthy and Sustainable Communities (2nd ed.) (pp. 43). San Francisco, CA: Redefining Progress.

[92] Kolko, Jo. (2012). Wicked Problems: Problems Worth Solving: A Handbook & A Call to Action. Austin, Tex: AC4D.

[93] Ridzi, Frank. Vice President, Community Investment. Central New York Community Foundation. (February 2, 2018). Telephone interview.

[94] Epstein, P. D., Coates, P. M., Wray, L. D., & Swain, D. (2006). Results that Matter: Improving Communities by Engaging Citizens, Measuring Performance, and Getting Things Done (pp. 39). San Francisco, CA: John Wiley & Sons.

[95] Epstein, P. D., Coates, P. M., Wray, L. D., & Swain, D. (2006). Results that Matter: Improving Communities by Engaging Citizens, Measuring Performance, and Getting Things Done (pp. 85). San Francisco, CA: John Wiley & Sons.

[96] Epstein, P. D., Coates, P. M., Wray, L. D., & Swain, D. (2006). Results that Matter: Improving Communities by Engaging Citizens, Measuring Performance, and Getting Things Done (pp. 116). San Francisco, CA: John Wiley & Sons.

[97] Community Tool Box. (2017). MAPP: Mobilizing for Action through Planning and Partnerships. Center for Community Health and Development at the University of Kansas. Retrieved from http://ctb.ku.edu/en/table-of-contents/overview/models-for-community-health-and-development/mapp/main

[98] Kania, J., & Kramer, M. (2011). Collective Impact. Stanford Social Innovation Review, Winter 2011. Retrieved from https://ssir.org/articles/entry/collective_impact

[99] Juster, J. S. (2017). Collective Impact. In Community Tool Box. Center for Community Health and Development at the University of Kansas. Retrieved from http://ctb.ku.edu/en/table-of-contents/overview/models-for-community-health-and-development/collective-impact/main

[100] Hanleybrown, F., Kania, J., & Kramer, M. (2012). Channeling Change: Making Collective Impact Work. Stanford Social Innovation Review. Retrieved from https://ssir.org/articles/entry/channeling_change_making_collective_impact_work

[101] Ibid.

[102] Juster, J. S. (2017). Collective Impact. In Community Tool Box. Retrieved from http://ctb.ku.edu/en/table-of-contents/overview/models-for-community-health-and-development/collective-impact/main

[103] Uribe, D., Wendel, C., & Bockstette, V. (2017). How to Lead Collective Impact Working Groups. FSG. Retrieved from https://collectiveimpactforum.org/sites/default/files/How%20to%20Lead%20Collective%20Impact%20Working%20Groups.pdf

[104] Juster, J. S. (2017). Collective Impact. In Community Tool Box. Center for Community Health and Development at the University of Kansas. Retrieved from http://ctb.ku.edu/en/table-of-contents/overview/models-for-community-health-and-development/collective-impact/main

[105] Epstein, P. D., Coates, P. M., Wray, L. D., & Swain, D. (2006). Results that Matter: Improving Communities by Engaging Citizens, Measuring Performance, and Getting Things Done. San Francisco, CA: John Wiley & Sons.

[106] NACCHO. (n.d.). Mobilizing for Action through Planning and Partnerships (MAPP) | NACCHO. Retrieved October 22, 2017, from http://archived.naccho.org/topics/infrastructure/Mapp/index.cfm

[107] Community Tool Box. (2017). MAPP: Mobilizing for Action through Planning and Partnerships. Retrieved October 11, 2017, from http://ctb.ku.edu/en/table-of-contents/overview/models-for-community-health-and-development/mapp/main

[108] Nagy, J., & Axner, M. (n.d.). Generating and Choosing Solutions. Retrieved February 20, 2018, from https://ctb.ku.edu/en/table-of-contents/analyze/analyze-community-problems-and-solutions/generate-solutions/main

[109] Community Tool Box. (2018). MAPP: Mobilizing for Action through Planning and Partnerships. Retrieved April 17, 2018, from https://ctb.ku.edu/en/table-of-contents/overview/models-for-community-health-and-development/mapp/main

[110] Collective Impact Forum. (n.d.). Work Group Action Planning Template. Retrieved January 10, 2018, from https://collectiveimpactforum.org/resources/work-group-action-planning-template

[111] Sharpe, M., & Combs, S. (November, 2017). Using Resident Data and Participation to Inform Agency and Broader Community Development. Presented at the 2017 Community Indicators Consortium Impact Summit. Retrieved from https://schd.ws/hosted_files/2017impactsummit/16/2017_St.Pete_Sharp_Combs_Potential_Unleashed.pdf

[112] Chapter 8. Developing a Strategic Plan | Section 5. Developing an Action Plan. Community Tool Box. (2017). Retrieved October 18, 2017, from http://ctb.ku.edu/en/table-of-contents/structure/strategic-planning/develop-action-plans/main

[113] University of Wisconsin Population Health Institute. (2017). County Health Rankings & Roadmaps Action Center. Retrieved February 26, 2018, from http://www.countyhealthrankings.org/take-action-improve-health/action-center

[114] Chapter 8. Developing a Strategic Plan | Section 5. Developing an Action Plan. Community Tool Box. (2017). Retrieved October 18, 2017, from http://ctb.ku.edu/en/table-of-contents/structure/strategic-planning/develop-action-plans/main

[115] Fawcett, S. B., Schultz, J., Francisco, V., Cyprus, J., Collie, V., Carson, V., & Bremby, R. (2001). Promoting Urban Neighborhood Development: An action planning guide for improving housing, jobs, education, safety and health, and human development. KU Workgroup on Health Promotion & Community Development. Retrieved from http://ctb.ku.edu/sites/default/files/chapter_files/promoting_urban_neighborhood_development.sflb_.pdf

[116] ABCD Institute. (2017). Asset-Based Community Development. Retrieved from https://resources.depaul.edu/abcd-institute/resources/Documents/ABCD%20DP%20Slide%20Presentation%20Descriptions.pdf

[117] Community Tool Box. (2017). MAPP: Mobilizing for Action through Planning and Partnerships. Center for Community Health and Development at the University of Kansas. Retrieved from http://ctb.ku.edu/en/table-of-contents/overview/models-for-community-health-and-development/mapp/main

[118] Cox, Molly. Better Know a Community Indicators Project Webinar: San Antonio SA2020 (July 15, 2016) Retrieved 2/3/2018 from http://communityindicators.net/knowledge/better-know-a-community-indicators-project-webinar-recordings/

[119] Epstein, P. D., Coates, P. M., Wray, L. D., & Swain, D. (2006). Results that Matter: Improving Communities by Engaging Citizens, Measuring Performance, and Getting Things Done (pp. 99). San Francisco, CA: John Wiley & Sons.

[120] Epstein, P. D., Coates, P. M., Wray, L. D., & Swain, D. (2006). Results that Matter: Improving Communities by Engaging Citizens, Measuring Performance, and Getting Things Done (pp. 202). San Francisco, CA: John Wiley & Sons.

[121] Bowie, P., Hargreaves, M., Joo, S., Boynton-Jarrett, R., Schneider, T., & Welch, L. (2017). A Peer Learning Approach to Improving Place Based Initiatives Measurement. Retrieved from https://2017impactsummit.sched.com/event/BqCg/pbi-5-a-peer-learning-approach-to-improving-place-based-initiatives-measurement. See also: https://schd.ws/hosted_files/2017impactsummit/ea/Peer%20Learning%20Panel%20Final%2011.15.17%20-%20Reduced.pdf

[122] Epstein, P. D., Coates, P. M., Wray, L. D., & Swain, D. (2006). Results that Matter: Improving Communities by Engaging Citizens, Measuring Performance, and Getting Things Done (pp. 113). San Francisco, CA: John Wiley & Sons.

[123] Epstein, P. D., Coates, P. M., Wray, L. D., & Swain, D. (2006). Results that Matter: Improving Communities by Engaging Citizens, Measuring Performance, and Getting Things Done (pp. 106). San Francisco, CA: John Wiley & Sons.

[124] Ibid.

[125] Ibid.

[126] Franz, N. (2013). The Data Party: Involving Stakeholders in Meaningful Data Analysis. Journal of Extension, 1IAW2.

[127] National Cancer Institute. (2011). Making Data Talk: A Workbook. Bethesda, MD: National Cancer Institute. Retrieved from https://www.cancer.gov/publications/health-communication/making-data-talk.pdf

[128] Rocha, H., & Miles, R. (2009). A Model of Collaborative Entrepreneurship for a More Humanistic Management. Journal of Business Ethics, 88(3), 445–462. https://doi.org/10.1007/s10551-009-0127-8

[129] Helmstetter, C., Mattessich, P., Hamberg, R., & Hartzler, N. (2017). Collaboration to Promote Use of Community Indicators: Communication Is Key. In Community Quality-of-Life Indicators: Best Cases VII (pp. 53–68). Springer, Cham. https://doi.org/10.1007/978-3-319-54618-6_4

[130] Ridzi, Frank. Vice President, Community Investment Central New York Community Foundation. (February 2, 2018). Telephone interview.

[131] Frey, B., Lohmeier, J., Lee, S., Tollefson, N. (2006). Measuring Collaboration Among Grant Partners. American Journal of Evaluation, 37(3), 383-392. https://doi.org/10.1177/1098214006290356 https://doi.org/10.1177/1098214006290356

[132] Hogue, T. (1993). Community-based collaboration: Community wellness multiplied. Bend, OR: Chandler Center for Community Leadership. Retrieved August 10, 2018, from http://www.uvm.edu/crs/nnco/collab/wellness.html

[133] Strategic Spartanburg. (n.d.). Spartanburg Community Indicators Project. Retrieved January 30, 2018, from http://www.strategicspartanburg.org/about/

[134] Strategic Spartanburg. (n.d.). Spartanburg Community Indicators Project. Retrieved July 30, 2018, from http://www.strategicspartanburg.org/about/scip-structure/

[135] Liuzzi, Allison. Project Director, Minnesota Compass. (January 24, 2018). Telephone interview.

[136] Tuckman, B. and Jensen, M. (1977). Stages of Small Group Development Revisited. Group and Organization Management, 2(4), 419-427.

[137] Joo, Sam. Director, Magnolia Community Initiative. (February 9, 2018). Telephone interview.

[138] Helmstetter, C., Mattessich, P., Hamberg, R., & Hartzler, N. (2017). Collaboration to Promote Use of Community Indicators: Communication Is Key. In Community Quality-of-Life Indicators: Best Cases VII (pp. 53–68). Springer, Cham. https://doi.org/10.1007/978-3-319-54618-6_4

[139] Temmer, Jennifer. Project Officer, International Institute for Sustainable Development; Team Lead, Peg. (February 8, 2018). Phone interview.

[140] Johnson, Ann. Senior Director, ACT Rochester. (January 30 2018). Telephone interview.

[141] Kania, J., & Kramer, M. (2011). Collective Impact. Stanford Social Innovation Review, Winter 2011. Retrieved from http://c.ymcdn.com/sites/www.lano.org/resource/dynamic/blogs/20131007_093137_25993.pdf

[142] Kania, J., & Kramer, M. (2011). Collective Impact. Stanford Social Innovation Review, Winter 2011. Retrieved from http://c.ymcdn.com/sites/www.lano.org/resource/dynamic/blogs/20131007_093137_25993.pdf

160

143 Collaboration for Impact. (n.d.). The Collective Impact Framework. Retrieved from

http://www.collaborationforimpact.com/collective-impact/

144 Truckee Meadows Healthy Communities. (2015). Collective Impact Reading Packet. Retrieved from
https://www.buildhealthyplaces.org/content/uploads/2017/05/Collective-Impact-Packet.pdf

145 The Collective Impact Framework | Collaboration for Impact. (n.d.). Retrieved August 22, 2018, from
https://www.collaborationforimpact.com/collective-impact/

146 Collaboration for Impact. (n.d.). The four phases of Collective Impact. Retrieved from
http://www.collaborationforimpact.com/the-how-to-guide/the-mindset-and-leadership-needed-2/

147 Hanleybrown, F., Kania, J., & Kramer, M. (2012). Channeling Change: Making Collective Impact Work.
Stanford Social Innovation Review. Retrieved from
https://ssir.org/articles/entry/channeling_change_making_collective_impact_work

148 Ridzi, Frank. Vice President, Community Investment Central New York Community Foundation. (February 2,
2018). Telephone interview.

149 Mattessich, P. (2001). Collaboration: What Makes It Work, 2nd Edition: A Review of Research Literature on
Factors Influencing Successful Collaboration. Amherst H. Wilder Foundation.

150 Helmstetter, C., Mattessich, P., Hamberg, R., & Hartzler, N. (2017). Collaboration to Promote Use of
Community Indicators: Communication Is Key. In Community Quality-of-Life Indicators: Best Cases VII (pp. 53–
68). Springer, Cham. https://doi.org/10.1007/978-3-319-54618-6_4

151 Ridzi, Frank. Vice President, Community Investment Central New York Community Foundation. (February 2,
2018). Telephone interview.

152 Wei Skillern, J., Erlichman, D., and Sawyer D. (2015). The Most Impactful Leaders You've Never Heard Of
(Stanford Social Innovation Review). Retrieved from
https://ssir.org/articles/entry/the_most_impactful_leaders_youve_never_heard_of

153 Iyer, Seema, Associate Director, Jacob France Institute; Director, Baltimore Neighborhood Indicators Alliance.
(January 31, 2018). Telephone interview.

154 Joo, Sam. Director, Magnolia Community Initiative. (February 9, 2018). Telephone interview.

155 Rubin, Hank. (2009). Collaborative Leadership: Developing Effective Partnerships for Communities and
Schools. Corwin Press.

156 Wei Skillern, J., Erlichman, D., and Sawyer D. (2015). The Most Impactful Leaders You've Never Heard Of
(Stanford Social Innovation Review). [Words attributed to Dr. Martin Luther King, Jr]. Retrieved from
https://ssir.org/articles/entry/the_most_impactful_leaders_youve_never_heard_of

157 Iyer, Seema, Associate Director, Jacob France Institute; Director, Baltimore Neighborhood Indicators Alliance.
(January 31, 2018). Telephone interview.

158 Carter, M. M. (2006). The Importance of Collaborative Leadership in Achieving Effective Criminal Justice
Outcomes. Center for Effective Public Policy. Retrieved from
http://www.collaborativejustice.org/docs/The%20Importance%20of%20Collaborative%20Leadership.doc

159 Ibid

160 Senge, P., Hamilton, H., & Kania, J. (2015). The dawn of system leadership. Stanford Social Innovation
Review, 13(1), 27-33. Retrieved from https://ssir.org/articles/entry/the_dawn_of_system_leadership

161 Ibid

162 Temmer, Jennifer. Project Officer, International Institute for Sustainable Development; Team Lead, Peg. (February 8, 2018). Phone interview.

163 Joo, Sam. Director, Magnolia Community Initiative. (February 9, 2018). Telephone interview.

164 Liuzzi, Allison. Project Director, Minnesota Compass. (January 24, 2018). Telephone interview.

165 William T. Grant Foundation. Communicating and Using Research Findings. Accessed December 2017. http://rpp.wtgrantfoundation.org/communicating-and-using-research-findings/answers

166 Lavis, J., Robertson, D., Woodside, J., McLeod, C., and Abelson, J. (2003). How Can Research Organizations More Effectively Transfer Research Knowledge to Decision Makers? The Milbank Quarterly 81:2. https://www.ncbi.nlm.nih.gov/pmc/articles/PMC2690219/

167 Johnson, Ann. Senior Director, ACT Rochester. (January 30 2018). Telephone interview.

168 Lavis, J., Robertson, D., Woodside, J., McLeod, C., and Abelson, J. (2003). How Can Research Organizations More Effectively Transfer Research Knowledge to Decision Makers? The Milbank Quarterly 81:2. https://www.ncbi.nlm.nih.gov/pmc/articles/PMC2690219/

169 Ibid

170 Mendonca, L. and Miller, M. (2007). Crafting a Message that sticks: An interview with Chip Heath. The McKinsey Quarterly. November 2007. Accessed December 2017. http://rpp.wtgrantfoundation.org/library/uploads/2016/01/Crafting-a-message-that-sticks.pdf

171 Temmer, Jennifer. Project Officer, International Institute for Sustainable Development; Team Lead, Peg. (February 8, 2018). Phone interview.

172 Weiss, C. (1979). The Many Meanings of Research Utilization. Public Administration Review 39:5, 426-431. http://crahd.phi.org/readings/Weiss1979ManyMeanings.pdf

173 Lavis, J., Robertson, D., Woodside, J., McLeod, C., and Abelson, J. (2003). How Can Research Organizations More Effectively Transfer Research Knowledge to Decision Makers? The Milbank Quarterly 81:2. https://www.ncbi.nlm.nih.gov/pmc/articles/PMC2690219/

174 National Cancer Institute. (2011). Making Data Talk: Communicating Public Health Data to the Public, Policy Makers, and the Press. National Institute of Health. https://www.cancer.gov/publications/health-communication/

175 Canadian Health Services Research Foundation. (2000). How to Give a Research Presentation to Decision-makers. http://rpp.wtgrantfoundation.org/library/uploads/2016/01/How-to-give-a-research-presentation-to-decision-makers.pdf

176 Moz. The Free Beginner's Guide to Social Media. Accessed December 2017. https://moz.com/beginners-guide-to-social-media

177 Johnson, Ann. Senior Director, ACT Rochester. (January 30 2018). Telephone interview.

178 Krug, S. (2014). Don't Make Me Think, Revisited: A Common Sense Approach to Web Usability. New Riders: Berkeley, California.

179 World Wide Web Consortium (W3C). (2018). Accessibility. Retrieved May 30, 2018, from https://www.w3.org/standards/webdesign/accessibility

180 Luetke, Michelle. (February 2, 2018). Better Know a Community Indicators Project CIC webinar: Santa Cruz County Community Assessment Project. http://communityindicators.net/knowledge/better-know-a-community-indicators-project-webinar-recordings/

[181] Lavis, J., Robertson, D., Woodside, J., McLeod, C., and Abelson, J. (2003). How Can Research Organizations More Effectively Transfer Research Knowledge to Decision Makers? The Milbank Quarterly 81:2. https://www.ncbi.nlm.nih.gov/pmc/articles/PMC2690219/

[182] Epstein, P. D., Coates, P. M., Wray, L. D., & Swain, D. (2006). *Results that matter: Improving communities by engaging citizens, measuring performance, and getting things done*. John Wiley & Sons. pp. 105

[183] Roberts, N. (2004). Public Deliberation in an Age of Direct Citizen Participation. The American Review of Public Administration, 34(4), 315–353. https://doi.org/10.1177/0275074004269288

[184] Lee, D. and H. Newby. (1983). The Problem of Sociology: An Introduction to the Discipline. (Unwin Hyman, London).

[185] Burby, R. J. (2003). Making Plans that Matter: Citizen Involvement and Government Action. Journal of the American Planning Association, 69(1), 33–49. https://doi.org/10.1080/01944360308976292

[186] Staley, K. Exploring impact: public involvement in NHS, public health and social care research. Eastleigh, United Kingdom: INVOLVE; 2009. [Cited in Principles of Community Engagement, CDC]

[187] Rowe, G., & Frewer, L. J. (2005). A Typology of Public Engagement Mechanisms. Science, Technology, & Human Values, 30(2), 251–290.

[188] Ministry of Social Development, New Zealand Government. (2007). The Basics: Degrees of Participation (Wellington, New Zealand).

[189] International Association for Public Participation. (2007). IAP2 Spectrum of Public Participation (Westminster, CO). https://iap2usa.org/resources/Documents/Core%20Values%20Awards/IAP2%20-%20Spectrum%20-%20stand%20alone%20document.pdf

[190] Wilcox, D. (1994). The Guide to Effective Participation (Joseph Rowntree Foundation, London).

[191] Hashagan, S. (2002). Models of Community Engagement (Scottish Community Development Centre, Scotland).

[192] Rowe, G., & Frewer, L. J. (2005). A Typology of Public Engagement Mechanisms. Science, Technology, & Human Values, 30(2), 251–290.

[193] Bowen, F., Newenham-Kahindi, A., & Herremans, I. (2010). When Suits Meet Roots: The Antecedents and Consequences of Community Engagement Strategy. Journal of Business Ethics, 95(2), 297–318. https://doi.org/10.1007/s10551-009-0360-1

[194] International Association for Public Participation. (2007). IAP2 Spectrum of Public Participation (Westminster, CO). https://iap2usa.org/resources/Documents/Core%20Values%20Awards/IAP2%20-%20Spectrum%20-%20stand%20alone%20document.pdf

[195] Hruby, Karen. Past Executive Director, Truckee Meadows Tomorrow. (February 9, 2018). Telephone interview.

[196] Innes, J. (1994) Growth management consensus project, in: J. Innes, J. Gruber, M. Neuman & R. Thompson (Eds) Coordinating Growth and Environmental Management Through Consensus Building, California Policy Seminar. CPS Report: A Policy Research Program Report, pp. 71–81 (Berkeley, CA, University of California).

[197] Innes, J.E. & Connick, S. (1999). San Francisco estuary project, in: L. Susskind, S. McKearnan & J. Thomas-Larmer (Eds) The Consensus Building Handbook: A Comprehensive Guide to Reaching Agreement (Thousand Oaks, CA, Sage Publications).

[198] Innes, J. E., & Booher, D. E. (2004). Reframing public participation: strategies for the 21st century. Planning Theory & Practice, 5(4), 419–436. https://doi.org/10.1080/1464935042000293170

[199] Ibid.

[200] Butterfoss, F. D. (2006). Process Evaluation for Community Participation. Annual Review of Public Health, 27, 323–340. http://www.annualreviews.org/doi/abs/10.1146/annurev.publhealth.27.021405.102207

[201] CDC. (2011). Principles of Community Engagement - Second Edition. https://www.atsdr.cdc.gov/communityengagement/pdf/PCE_Report_508_FINAL.pdf

[202] Epstein, P. D., Coates, P. M., Wray, L. D., & Swain, D. (2006). *Results that matter: Improving communities by engaging citizens, measuring performance, and getting things done.* John Wiley & Sons. pp. 113.

[203] Head, B. W. (2007). Community Engagement: Participation on Whose Terms? Australian Journal of Political Science, 42(3), 441–454. https://doi.org/10.1080/10361140701513570

[204] Innes, J. E., Gruber, J., Thompson, R., and Neuman, M. (1994). Coordinating Growth and Environmental Management through Consensus Building. Berkeley, CA: California Policy Seminar, University of California.

[205] Burby, R. J. (2003). Making Plans that Matter: Citizen Involvement and Government Action. Journal of the American Planning Association, 69(1), 33–49. https://doi.org/10.1080/01944360308976292

[206] Yankelovich, D. (2001). Choosing Our Future: How Citizens Envision the Growth of the San Diego Region. A Final Report to The William and Flora Hewlett Foundation (La Jolla, CA, University of California San Diego).

[207] Gruber, J. (1994) Coordinating Growth Management Through Consensus-Building: Incentives and the Generation of Social, Intellectual, and Political Capital. Working Paper No. 617 (Berkeley, CA, Institute of Urban and Regional Development, University of California at Berkeley).

[208] Arnstein, S. R. (1969). A Ladder Of Citizen Participation. Journal of the American Institute of Planners, 35(4), 216–224. https://doi.org/10.1080/01944366908977225

[209] CDC. (2011). Principles of Community Engagement - Second Edition. https://www.atsdr.cdc.gov/communityengagement/pdf/PCE_Report_508_FINAL.pdf

[210] Wallerstein, N. B., & Duran, B. (2006). Using Community-Based Participatory Research to Address Health Disparities. Health Promotion Practice, 7(3), 312–323. https://doi.org/10.1177/1524839906289376

[211] Luetke, Michelle (February 2, 2018). Better Know a Community Indicators Project CIC webinar: Santa Cruz County Community Assessment Project. http://communityindicators.net/knowledge/better-know-a-community-indicators-project-webinar-recordings/

[212] Epstein, P. D., Coates, P. M., Wray, L. D., & Swain, D. (2006). *Results that matter: Improving communities by engaging citizens, measuring performance, and getting things done.* John Wiley & Sons. pp. 19

[213] Epstein, P. D., Coates, P. M., Wray, L. D., & Swain, D. (2006). *Results that matter: Improving communities by engaging citizens, measuring performance, and getting things done.* John Wiley & Sons. pp. 21

[214] Epstein, P. D., Coates, P. M., Wray, L. D., & Swain, D. (2006). *Results that matter: Improving communities by engaging citizens, measuring performance, and getting things done.* John Wiley & Sons. pp. 27-32

[215] Epstein, P. D., Coates, P. M., Wray, L. D., & Swain, D. (2006). *Results that matter: Improving communities by engaging citizens, measuring performance, and getting things done.* John Wiley & Sons.

[216] Cox, M. (2016) Better Know a Community Indicator Project – SA2020. http://www.communityindicators.net/publications/show/140

[217] Joo, Sam. Director, Magnolia Community Initiative. (February 9, 2018). Telephone interview.

[218] SA2020. (2018). FAQs | SA2020. Retrieved January 14, 2018, from https://www.sa2020.org/faqs/

[219] Children's Bureau. (n.d.). Magnolia Place Community Initiative – Sustaining community health and well-being. Retrieved May 30, 2018, from http://magnoliaplacela.org/

[220] JCCI. (2015). JCCI Jacksonville Community Council, Inc. Retrieved April 5, 2018, from http://jcciweb.wixsite.com/jcci

[221] Epstein, P. D., Coates, P. M., Wray, L. D., & Swain, D. (2006). *Results that matter: Improving communities by engaging citizens, measuring performance, and getting things done*. John Wiley & Sons.

[222] Hruby, Karen. Truckee Meadows Tomorrow. (February 9, 2018).Telephone interview.

[223] Epstein, P. D., Coates, P. M., Wray, L. D., & Swain, D. (2006). *Results that matter: Improving communities by engaging citizens, measuring performance, and getting things done*. John Wiley & Sons.

[224] Truckee Meadows Tomorrow. (2015). A Brief History of the Organization. Retrieved May 30, 2018, from https://www.truckeemeadowstomorrow.org/about-us/history/

[225] Roberts, N. (2004). Public Deliberation in an Age of Direct Citizen Participation. The American Review of Public Administration, 34(4), 315–353. https://doi.org/10.1177/0275074004269288

[226] Roberts, N. (2004). Public Deliberation in an Age of Direct Citizen Participation. The American Review of Public Administration, 34(4), p. 332. https://doi.org/10.1177/0275074004269288

[227] Bassler, A., Brasiser, K., Fogle, N., & Taverno, R. (2008). Developing effective citizen engagement: A how-to guide for community Leaders." Center for Rural America.

[228] Epstein, P. D., Coates, P. M., Wray, L. D., & Swain, D. (2006). *Results that matter: Improving communities by engaging citizens, measuring performance, and getting things done*. John Wiley & Sons., p 119.

[229] Iyer, Seema, Associate Director, Jacob France Institute; Director, Baltimore Neighborhood Indicators Alliance. (January 31, 2018). Telephone interview.

[230] Anderson, B., & Paton, D. (2004). Creating Welcoming Places Workbook. Community Activators. Retrieved from https://resources.depaul.edu/abcd-institute/resources/Documents/WelcomWorkbook_final.pdf

[231] Joo, S. (2017). Building a Measurement System for Place Based Initiatives. Panel discussion at the Community Indicators Project Impact Summit.

[232] U.S. Census Bureau. (n.d.). American FactFinder - Community Facts. Retrieved December 13, 2017, from https://factfinder.census.gov/faces/nav/jsf/pages/community_facts.xhtml

[233] Tamarack Institute. (2018). Who do we want to engage? Tool. Retrieved January 22, 2018, from https://www.tamarackcommunity.ca/hubfs/Resources/Tools/Who%20do%20we%20want%20to%20engage%20tool.pdf

[234] Community Tool Box. (n.d.). Increasing Participation and Membership. Retrieved October 17, 2017, from http://ctb.ku.edu/en/increasing-participation-and-membership

[235] Rabinowitz, P. (n.d.). Participatory Approaches to Planning Community Interventions. Retrieved November 3, 2017, from http://ctb.ku.edu/en/table-of-contents/analyze/where-to-start/participatory-approaches/main

[236] Anderson, B., & Paton, D. (2004). Creating Welcoming Places Workbook. Community Activators. Retrieved from https://resources.depaul.edu/abcd-institute/resources/Documents/WelcomWorkbook_final.pdf

[237] Kramer, R. for Community Tool Box. (2018). Developing a Plan for Increasing Participation in Community Action. Retrieved May 30, 2018, from https://ctb.ku.edu/en/table-of-contents/participation/encouraging-involvement/increase-participation/main

[238] Colorado Association of School Boards. (n.d.). Sample Invitation Email. Retrieved November 1, 2017, from https://www.casb.org/site/default.aspx?PageType=3&ModuleInstanceID=381&ViewID=7b97f7ed-8e5e-4120-848f-a8b4987d588f&RenderLoc=0&FlexDataID=393&PageID=291

[239] Tamarack Institute. (n.d.). Index of Community Engagement Techniques. Retrieved November 3, 2017, from https://cdn2.hubspot.net/hubfs/316071/Resources/Tools/Index%20of%20Engagement%20Techniques.pdf

[240] Ibid.

[241] Elkins, L. A., Bivins, D., & Holbrook, L. (2009). Community Visioning Process: A Tool for Successful Planning. *Journal of Higher Education Outreach and Engagement, 13*(4), 75-84.

[242] National Co-ordinating Centre for Public Engagement. (2017). How to perform participatory mapping. Retrieved September 12, 2017, from https://www.publicengagement.ac.uk/sites/default/files/publication/how_to_perform_participatory_mapping.pdf

[243] Bassler, A., Brasier, K., Fogle, N., & Taverno, R. (2008). Developing Effective Citizen Engagement: A How-to Guide for Community Leaders. Center for Rural Pennsylvania. Retrieved from http://www.rural.palegislature.us/Effective_Citizen_Engagement.pdf

[244] Rabinowitz, P. (n.d.). Participatory Approaches to Planning Community Interventions. Retrieved November 3, 2017, from http://ctb.ku.edu/en/table-of-contents/analyze/where-to-start/participatory-approaches/main

[245] Community Tool Box. (n.d.). Increasing Participation and Membership. Retrieved October 17, 2017, from http://ctb.ku.edu/en/increasing-participation-and-membership

[246] Anderson, B., & Paton, D. (2004). Creating Welcoming Spaces Workbook (ABCD Toolkit). Community Activators. Retrieved from https://resources.depaul.edu/abcd-institute/resources/Documents/WelcomWorkbook_final.pdf

[247] Rabinowitz, P. (n.d.). Participatory Approaches to Planning Community Interventions. Retrieved November 3, 2017, from http://ctb.ku.edu/en/table-of-contents/analyze/where-to-start/participatory-approaches/main

[248] Ibid.

[249] Juster, J. S. (2017). Collective Impact. In Community Tool Box. Retrieved from http://ctb.ku.edu/en/table-of-contents/overview/models-for-community-health-and-development/collective-impact/main

[250] Nagy, J., & Axner, M. (2017). Analyzing Community Problems and Solutions. Retrieved March 18, 2018, from https://ctb.ku.edu/en/table-of-contents/analyze/analyze-community-problems-and-solutions/generate-solutions/main